T0323987

Cambridge Elements ☰

Elements in Historical Theory and Practice
edited by
Daniel Woolf
Queen's University, Ontario

A HUMAN RIGHTS VIEW OF THE PAST

Antoon De Baets
University of Groningen

CAMBRIDGE
UNIVERSITY PRESS

Shaftesbury Road, Cambridge CB2 8EA, United Kingdom

One Liberty Plaza, 20th Floor, New York, NY 10006, USA

477 Williamstown Road, Port Melbourne, VIC 3207, Australia

314–321, 3rd Floor, Plot 3, Splendor Forum, Jasola District Centre, New Delhi – 110025, India

103 Penang Road, #05–06/07, Visioncrest Commercial, Singapore 238467

Cambridge University Press is part of Cambridge University Press & Assessment, a department of the University of Cambridge.

We share the University's mission to contribute to society through the pursuit of education, learning and research at the highest international levels of excellence.

www.cambridge.org
Information on this title: www.cambridge.org/9781009547857

DOI: 10.1017/9781009345927

First published 2024

A catalogue record for this publication is available from the British Library

ISBN 978-1-009-54785-7 Hardback
ISBN 978-1-009-34594-1 Paperback
ISSN 2634-8616 (online)
ISSN 2634-8608 (print)

A Human Rights View of the Past

Elements in Historical Theory and Practice

DOI: 10.1017/9781009345927
First published online: December 2024

Antoon De Baets
University of Groningen

Author for correspondence: Antoon De Baets, a.h.m.de.baets@rug.nl

Abstract: The idea of human rights has been much criticized from a historical perspective but curiously enough its theoretical and practical contributions to the study of time, memory, and history have never been systematically explored. How is it to look at the past from a human rights perspective? How can historical writing benefit from applying a human rights logic? In tackling these questions, the Element first clarifies what a human rights view of the past is. The constituent dimensions of the past – time, memory, and history – are then reviewed, indicating what a human rights perspective can add to the study of each. Finally, the benefits accruing from a human rights view of the past to historical theory and practice are highlighted.

Keywords: freedom of expression, international law, memorialization, responsible history, time regimes

ISBNs: 9781009547857 (HB), 9781009345941 (PB), 9781009345927 (OC)
ISSNs: 2634-8616 (online), 2634-8608 (print)

Contents

Introduction

This Element springs from a deep concern: Human rights are in crisis and yet their rich potential for understanding our time has not been fully explored.[1]

Since their conceptual birth in the early Enlightenment, human rights have always been developed and defended against a background of ongoing atrocities and wars in which they were grossly violated. At the same time, conservative, liberal, and socialist thinkers argued against ascribing an abstract and absolute character to these human rights and maintained that they should be embedded in the societies in which they were exercised. After World War II – a war with unprecedented atrocities – the idea of human rights received a new impulse and, incorporating the early criticism, reinvented itself as the Universal Declaration of Human Rights of 1948, which became the flagship of a wave of human rights treaties.

Despite these impressive successes, the universality claim of human rights was regularly attacked, for example by Asian heads of state who in the 1990s defended the existence of "Asian values,"[2] or in 2009–2013 when a heterogenous group of United Nations Member States launched a campaign to revalorize "traditional values."[3] In some corners of the world, autocrats and populists questioned the notion of human rights itself. Since 2015 the very idea of human rights has come under sustained attack, with some even talking about a "post-human-rights world" and denying the validity of the notion of human rights altogether. It is a fact that the leaders of several major powers have tried to formulate alternatives to Western geopolitical dominance, alternatives in which human rights play a minor role or are replaced by regional values or *raison d'état*.

I do not share this uncritical opposition against the universality of human rights. Starting with the Universal Declaration of Human Rights, all international human rights instruments have been drafted by diplomats and legal scholars from multiple backgrounds. The fact that the idea of human rights was originally developed in a Western context does not in itself disprove its applicability in other contexts. Furthermore, the claim that human rights are not universal has always been defended by political leaders and critics who relativize human rights in the name of non-Western communities and cultures, but never by non-Western victims of human rights violations who languish in the dictator's torture chambers themselves. Quite the opposite; whenever possible,

---

[1] The human rights crisis since ca. 2015, discussed in De Baets 2023a, 315–316.
[2] The Asian values debate, discussed in Sen, 13–16.
[3] The tradition debate, discussed in HRC, Preliminary; HRC, Promoting; HRC, Study; HRC, Summary; IMFE, Joint Declaration [Universality], §1a–h.

these victims have claimed their human rights with desperate voices. Denying the enjoyment of human rights to them in the name of community, culture, or tradition is, they argue, discriminatory, if not outright racist.

Whereas responsible criticism of human rights should be welcomed, destructive criticism does not help us much. This Element argues that we have not yet exploited the full potential of human rights. It explores that potential in one domain of existence, the past, and tries to answer two questions: How is it to look at the past from a human rights perspective? And how can historical writing benefit from applying human rights principles? In light of the proliferation of past-related activities since the advent of the internet, it is timely to highlight the beneficial uses of human rights for the study of the past. Before outlining my perspective, I should elucidate some approaches not adopted in this Element.

The present Element offers neither a conceptual nor a substantial history of human rights. Let me explain this. The expression "history of human rights" has two meanings. *Conceptually*, it is the history of the idea of human rights. Such a conceptual history typically starts with Enlightenment thought about the idea, casts a quick glance at its precursors in previous centuries and other cultures, and then traces the long and winding path of the idea up until today. *Substantively*, it is the history of human rights in practice, including their violations. Such a substantive history usually identifies periods of progress and failure in the compliance with human rights. The present Element offers neither of these approaches to the history of human rights.

Another approach not chosen is the one adopted by some Special Rapporteurs of the United Nations (further abbreviated as UN) – especially the UN Special Rapporteur in the field of cultural rights and the UN Special Rapporteur on truth, justice, and reparation. Around 2012 these rapporteurs became interested in issues of history, memory, and heritage, and started presenting reports about these topics to the UN General Assembly. The UN Special Rapporteur on cultural rights, for example, asked how historical narratives were relevant to human rights and how they could strengthen peace and respect for human rights rather than create divisions and tensions among different groups of society.[4]

This UN perspective is important, but this Element takes the opposite approach. My leading question is not how historical narratives are relevant to human rights but how human rights narratives are relevant to history. I look at the human rights principles agreed upon since 1948 and ask whether and how

---

[4] SRCR, History and Memorialisation.

they can enrich our understanding of the past. "Understanding the past" covers a wider field than historical writing alone: Its scope also extends to broader issues related to time and memory. I am keenly aware that human rights were never designed with the purpose of improving our understanding of the past and hence that reading them in this light contains a danger of mission creep. Therefore, I will proceed carefully and read human rights principles with the eyes of a historian and debates about historical writing with the eyes of a human rights scholar.

Sources

I will mainly explore human rights sources of an international and supranational scope and largely exclude their domestic or hybrid equivalents or variations – except where the latter provide strong illustrations of particular situations. In the domain of international human rights law, which protects the human rights of individuals at all times (in peacetime as well as in war), the so-called International Bill of Human Rights has unsurpassed authority. It consists of three instruments: the Universal Declaration of Human Rights (abbreviated as UDHR) from 1948, and the International Covenant on Civil and Political Rights (abbreviated as ICCPR) and the International Covenant on Economic, Social and Cultural Rights (abbreviated as ICESCR), both from 1966. The latter two are binding treaties derived from the UDHR: As of October 2024, 174 States had ratified the ICCPR and 172 the ICESCR. The UN Human Rights Committee and the UN Committee on Economic, Social and Cultural Rights oversee implementation of the ICCPR and ICESCR, respectively. Reports of these bodies, in particular their General Comments on the Covenants and their Communications (judgments on individual human rights complaints), were prioritized in the research for this Element. The International Bill of Human Rights is the main reference point throughout the Element.

The following sources are used to put forward *additional* arguments and claims. I consulted advisory opinions of the International Court of Justice (the so-called World Court belonging to the UN); judgments of regional human rights courts; and influential UN commentaries (for example, from the International Law Commission) and UN principles (for example, the Impunity Principles and Reparation Principles). In the domain of international humanitarian law, which protects the rights of individuals during armed conflicts, the Geneva Conventions of 1949 (universally ratified) and their Additional Protocols of 1977 were leading reference sources, as well as the rules of customary international law applicable in wartime (written down by the International Committee of the Red Cross in 2005). I also needed to look at the domain of international criminal law to study those violations of human rights that amount to crimes. Whereas international human rights law establishes *State* responsibility for human rights breaches, international criminal law establishes *individual* responsibility for three gross crimes: genocide, crimes against humanity, and war crimes. Since approximately 2005, these three crimes have often been referred to under the portmanteau formula "atrocity crimes."[5] The most important instrument in this domain is the Rome Statute of the International Criminal Court, approved in 1998.

In short, the following outline of a human rights view of the past is based on and inspired by instruments of international human rights, humanitarian, and criminal law that have stood the test of time and by and large received global and enduring endorsement. Those unfamiliar with legal approaches may want to read Section 2 (A Human Rights View of Time) last.

1 A Human Rights View of the Past

1.1 Definition

A human rights view of the past describes, analyzes, and evaluates events from the past through the prism of the principles of international human rights law. In order to construct such a view, it is imperative to perceive the past in its entirety, including its dark episodes marked by atrocity crimes which compel historians to pay attention to the taboos of history and areas shrouded in secrecy. A human rights view of the past suggests applying methodological and ethical principles to look at these events.

In terms of philosophy of history, a human rights inspired view of the past can be called a speculative philosophy of history (to the extent that it contains a view of the contours of history) as well as a critical philosophy of history (to the extent that it offers methodological and ethical clues for those examining the past). In terms of the history of ideas, a human rights inspired view of the past recognizes that ideas about how humanity should conduct its affairs in ethical ways are important forces in history. It does not assume, however, that ideas are the only engines of history: By recognizing economic, social, and cultural rights, which are only progressively achieved (Article 2.1 ICESCR), human rights draw systematic attention to processes and structures in history.

I assume that the human rights principles under discussion here are sufficiently coherent so as to justify speaking of *a* human rights view of the past. The purpose of this Element is to demonstrate that such a view of the past exists and to help solve real problems with issues of time, memory, and history more convincingly than otherwise would be the case.

---

[5] OGPRP, Framework.

1.2 Discussion

Each specific perspective on the past carries risks of distortion, and a human rights perspective of the past is no exception. In the following, I briefly distinguish several groups of such risks. All of them are serious, although, as we have seen, critics sometimes tend to exaggerate them:[6]

- *Scope risks.* The assumptions that rights are properties of human beings and that nonhuman sentient beings do not possess them (anthropocentrism); that human nature has an essence that resists evolutionary and historical change (essentialism); and that human rights are universal across space, despite their Western origins (universalism).
- *Perspective risks.* The tendency to exclusively focus on human rights violations and on the dark side of history while neglecting information about human rights improvements (leading to a catastrophic view of history).
- *Agency risks.* The assumption that individuals determine the course of events to the detriment of processual and structural factors and the tendency to coerce the complex personalities of these individuals into the straitjacket of human rights violations, that is, to see them merely as victims, perpetrators, or bystanders.
- *Teleological risks.* The tendency to view history as a path ineluctably leading from an initial situation of chaos and violence to the present situation of relative peace and human rights compliance.
- *Epistemological risks.* The tendency to reconceptualize historical crimes in contemporary legal terms and the risk of anachronism when these terms and associated values are impermissibly transferred to the past.
- *Heuristic risks.* The circumstance that victims of crimes usually leave fewer traces than perpetrators of crimes and that the latter tend to erase whatever crime traces remain, leading to a survivorship bias at the level of information sources.
- *Instrumentalization risks.* The tendency to de-historicize, moralize, and judicialize history and transform it into a platform for reparation claims of victim groups.

---

[6] The literature criticizing human rights is vast. The arguments against the human rights idea are mostly lucid but they sometimes suffer from the straw man fallacy (especially in far-fetched claims that human rights history is triumphalist, or elitist, or that it contains a misleading version of emancipation, or implies neoliberal bias). In addition, some authors are ahistorical in their surprise that not all drafters of human rights instruments acted with noble intentions all the time or that the history of the idea of human rights, like any history of ideas, has a dubious side. Even stripped of its suggestive iconoclasm, however, enough criticism remains to worry about. For some evaluations, see Kennedy 2002 and 2012; Halme-Tuomisaari and Slotte; Hoffmann; Salojärvi.

- *Propaganda risks.* The risk of abusing the human rights rhetoric to conceal or justify unequal power relations.[7]

These risks are real (and most apply to other perspectives on the past as well), but they do not necessarily materialize. If they do, they can be fatal, especially in combination. Awareness of these biases and risks is the first step in suspending them. Therefore, when exploring the possibilities of a human rights view in the following sections, we need to keep these risks at the back of our minds.

2 A Human Rights View of Time

The time dimension is the cornerstone of any view of the past, including a human rights view of the past. It constitutes the infrastructure for memory (with its telescopic view of time) and history (with its linear view of time). More specifically in our case, the temporal scope of a human rights view of the past has two distinctive features: It can be contracted, often severely, or expanded, often widely. The breadth of scope depends on the impact of legal principles and procedural rules on the duration of the relevant time under scrutiny. This is best seen in the field where crimes are adjudicated – international criminal law. The recent surge in interest in the concept of time within the historical profession has not yet fully appreciated the view of time that can be distilled from these legal principles and procedural rules.[8]

2.1 Time-Constraining Effects

Past-oriented effects. When victims of human rights violations bring their complaints before the court, some principles and rules restrict the scope of these complaints backward. The most important is the *nonretroactivity principle*, which prescribes that laws and treaties cannot be imposed retroactively. This is a basic principle in any system based on the rule of law, and, therefore, it is a key provision in the treaty that governs treaties: the Vienna Convention on the Law of Treaties.[9] The principle is also formulated in Article 15 ICCPR. First mentioned in the Constitution of the United States and the French Déclaration des droits de l'homme et du citoyen, both from 1789, it was conceptualized by Anselm von Feuerbach in 1801. Feuerbach coined the phrase under which the principle became famous in criminal law: *Nullum crimen, nulla poena sine praevia lege* ("No crime, no penalty without previous law"); an act cannot be

---

[7] UDHR Art. 30 warns against the abuse of human rights.

[8] The following is not an exhaustive analysis of time in international law. Many time-related principles (e.g., *vacatio legis, estoppel, laches, res judicata, stare decisis*) remain unmentioned here.

[9] VCLT, Art. 28.

criminal and should not be punished if no pre-existing law prohibited it.[10] The nonretroactivity principle is one of the most powerful principles in law because it provides legal certainty. However, it has an often overlooked international dimension: I will come back to this.

An application of the nonretroactivity principle is the rule of *ratione temporis* ("by reason of time"), prescribing that a complaint must relate to a breach which occurred *after* a human rights treaty or protocol under which the complaint was filed came into force for the State concerned, thus preventing a complaint from *before* that date from being heard or investigated. This date is called the *critical date*.

Future-oriented effects. The scope is also limited in the other direction. The *finality principle* guides litigation according to the maxim *Interest rei publicae ut finis litium sit* ("It is in the public interest that lawsuits have an end").[11] The reason behind this principle is that relevant evidence in a case sometimes gets lost and usually becomes unreliable over time, thus jeopardizing a fair trial (although new confessions or newly discovered evidence can never be excluded). Related to the finality principle and equally serving the fair trial purpose is the *prescription principle*, which stipulates that (most) crimes are subject to statutes of limitations or time bars, implying that they cannot be investigated or prosecuted anymore after a certain amount of time (differing from crime to crime) has elapsed. A special application of the finality principle is the maxim *Actio personalis moritur cum persona* ("Personal action dies with the person concerned"), meaning that a prosecution stops when the suspect dies – in sharp contrast to the research of historians, which never stops at the deaths of its protagonists, and indeed often begins at that moment.

Along with these principles, a quasi-legal body such as the UN Human Rights Committee has adopted *additional time-sensitive rules* in dealing with individual complaints within the ICCPR framework. For example, the committee does not reassess findings of fact by domestic courts, even when the latter are based on contested historical records, unless these courts acted manifestly in an arbitrary way. In addition, the committee's complaints procedure is personal: It is designed for individuals claiming to have been the victim of a violation themselves. This means that an *actio popularis* (a complaint in the public interest) or a challenge of legal provisions deemed to be contrary to the ICCPR *in the abstract* is not admissible. It is not allowed, for example, to submit broad historical claims involving Article 1 ICCPR (the right to self-determination, which is a collective right). Thus, the purpose of human rights bodies is not to redress all the injustices of history.

---

[10] Mokhtar, 46. See also ECtHR, Guide.   [11] Higgins, 511–515.

Past- and future-oriented effects. A factor that restricts the temporal scope in both directions is the granting of *victim status*. A victim status is required to file complaints. At the past-oriented side of the victim spectrum, most legal definitions of "victim" do not include dead persons. In particular, the 1985 UN Declaration of Basic Principles of Justice for Victims of Crime and Abuse of Power, which contains the most frequently used definition of victims, does not talk about the dead. It distinguishes direct victims, who are those suffering harm through crime or abuse of power, and indirect victims, meaning the immediate family of the direct victims and persons who suffer harm while trying to help direct victims.[12] But it is highly unlikely that "those suffering harm through crime" include the dead. Insofar as the declaration seems to include them, it emphasizes the role of their dependents.[13] At the future-oriented side of the victim spectrum, children who were alive at the time of a human rights violation suffered by their parents are more likely to be recognized as indirect victims than children born after these events or than grandchildren. In short, judicial victimhood seems to extend over two generations, the present and the next, and occasionally three (if grandchildren are taken into account).

The victim status is at the heart of current discussions about *transgenerational harm* at the International Criminal Court. In investigating this notion of transgenerational harm in a Congolese case, the court reasoned that traumas are individual, not collective. However, children of parents who have lived through traumatizing events (in this case, an armed attack on their village) could develop derivative traumas themselves by hearing the stories of survivors of those events. The court therefore recognized that children, including those born after the events, could suffer from transgenerational psychological harm, defined as "[A] phenomenon, whereby social violence is passed on from ascendants to descendants with traumatic consequences for the latter."[14] However, it did not grant reparations to the children in this particular case because the causal nexus between the harm they suffered and the attack on the village in which their parents were hit had not been sufficiently demonstrated according to the evidentiary standard of a balance of probabilities (meaning here that the court was not convinced that it was more likely than not that the attack had caused the harm).[15]

---

[12] In Reparation Principles, Art. 8, and Disappearance Convention, Art. 24.1, the term "indirect victim" is not used anymore.

[13] Victims Principles, Principles 1–2 (and 12b). See also Disappearance Declaration, Art. 19. For background, see De Baets 2023b, 28–29.

[14] ICC, Trial Chamber II, Order, §132.

[15] ICC, Trial Chamber II, Public Redacted Version, §140. ICC decisions regarding transgenerational harm are also underway in the Congolese case of Ntaganda (2020–) and the Ugandan case

A similar transgenerational trauma case, related to two persons who disappeared in 1936 (during the Spanish Civil War), was brought before the UN Human Rights Committee. In 2019 the granddaughter of the disappeared argued that for years her mother and her aunt had been unable to talk to her about the disappearances. When in 1975 she herself found out what happened, she understood that their ostensibly incomprehensible behavior was caused by a trauma. She further argued that she felt the effects of the trauma herself because the continuing denial of the disappearances on the part of the Spanish State prevented her from mourning. The committee eventually rejected her complaint but on different grounds: It argued that it had no jurisdiction *ratione temporis* as the principal events underlying the violation took place too far back before the critical date (Spain's ratification of the ICCPR in 1977).[16]

There is one other type of measures with both backward- and forward-oriented constraining effects: *amnesty laws*. Amnesty laws have the effect of *retroactively* nullifying previously established liability or sentences of perpetrators or *prospectively* barring prosecution of crime suspects.[17] Such amnesties are frequently applied in the context of transitional justice – the period during which a dictatorship gives way to an emergent democracy. In these transitional situations, the interest in peace (the interest in political stability after a divisive conflict) has to be balanced with the interest in justice (the interest in prosecuting atrocities committed during that conflict). In this balancing, the urge to forget and reconcile is often more powerful than the urge to remember and prosecute, especially in situations where massive violence has left the hands of many dirty.[18] Amnesties lead to legal forgetting and, sometimes, social forgetting. With one exception though: International criminal law prohibits the use of amnesty laws to obstruct the investigation of atrocity crimes.[19]

Amnesty laws in fact hamper the recovery of information because by nullifying liability or sentences, or halting or preventing investigation and prosecution, criminal records may be erased, remain incomplete, or never come into existence. This obstructs a fuller disclosure of how perpetrators committed their crimes and interferes with the right of their victims and of society at large to know the truth.[20] In addition, amnesties may negatively impact access to legal

---

of Ongwen (2022–). See also Loth, 206, distinguishing ancestor-based and descendant-based claims.

[16] CCPR, F.A.J. and B.M.R.A, §§2.11, 3.7, 7.6; see also CCPR, K.K. and others, Joint opinion of Committee members Brands Kehris and Bulkan (partly dissenting).

[17] Retroactively exempting convicted criminals from serving their sentences is a pardon. See OHCHR, Amnesties, 43, for definitions.

[18] Hazan, 8–10.

[19] ICC, Rome Statute, Art. 29; CCPR, General Comment 20, §15. See also Impunity Principles, Principle 24; OHCHR, Amnesties, passim; *Belfast Guidelines*, 52–53.

[20] OHCHR, Amnesties, 31, 33; *Belfast Guidelines*, 21, 52–55, 59.

records and even prevent historians from mentioning the crimes committed by those pardoned and amnestied or the verdicts meted out to them.[21]

We see that multiple principles and rules severely restrict the temporal scope of law and adjudication. In inventive and sometimes unexpected ways, however, the temporal horizon can be enlarged.

2.2 Time-Expanding Effects

Past-oriented effects. Some principles and rules have the potential to expand the temporal scope backward. A simple but very effective time-expanding tool is the following: When investigating a complaint, judges have the liberty to look at and assess events that occurred prior to the critical date,[22] and to apply *reasonings by analogy and precedent*,[23] to the extent that their interpretations of the further past shed light – contextual, causal, or otherwise – on the facts of the case.[24]

Another powerful procedural means to broaden the temporal scope of a case is to look at other *sources of international law* than treaties. The statute of the International Court of Justice stipulates that there are four sources of international law: international conventions (treaties), international custom, general principles of law recognized by the community of nations, and judicial decisions.[25] Of these, *international custom* in particular stretches time backward.[26] In the court's statute, custom is defined as "evidence of a general practice accepted as law."[27] Although there is no such thing as "instant custom," no particular duration is required to call a practice a custom.[28] The International Court of Justice can determine whether a given practice, including the practice flowing from a treaty rule, has acquired the status of customary international law and since when. Once a practice is recognized as such, all States are deemed bound by it, regardless of whether they have ratified the treaty in question.

---

[21] For an example, see De Baets 2016, 5–6.

[22] Under the rule of judicial notice, well-known historical facts can be introduced as evidence in court. In the Mermelstein case (see Superior Court of the State of California), e.g., the trial judge famously declared, in 1981: "Under Evidence Code Section 452(h), this court does take judicial notice of the fact that Jews were gassed to death at the Auschwitz Concentration Camp in Poland during the summer of 1944."

[23] ICC, Rome Statute, Art. 22.2, prohibits "legal creep": extending definitions of crimes by analogy. This prohibition, however, refers to analogy as a law-making tool, not to analogy as an interpretation tool.

[24] See also Sunstein (2014), 62–100; Sunstein (2023).

[25] ICJ, Statute, Art. 38.1. This article already appears in the statute of the Permanent Court of International Justice (the ICJ predecessor in operation 1922–46).

[26] Customary *international* law should not be confused with *local* dispute resolution based on custom.

[27] Probably, historians would conceptually prefer "tradition" over "custom."

[28] Identification, Annex, Conclusion 8.2.

Famously, customary international law played a crucial role in the proceedings before the International Military Tribunal at *Nuremberg*, when key Nazi leaders were prosecuted in 1946–8 for their crimes in World War II. The tribunal's jurisdiction only covered wartime events and therefore stretched back to 1939 – six years before its establishment.[29] When it was accused of administering retroactive justice because its 1945 Charter did not only list crimes that already existed in 1939 (notably war crimes) but also *new* crimes (namely crimes against peace and crimes against humanity),[30] the tribunal rejected the charge with two arguments. First, it pointed to a clause in its charter stating that, as an *international* tribunal, it would punish crimes against humanity "whether or not [committed] in violation of the domestic law of the country where perpetrated." Second, in its judgment, it argued that its charter – including that clause – was "the expression of international law existing at the time of its creation [1945]" and that "individuals ha[d] international duties which transcend[ed] the national obligations of obedience imposed by the individual state."[31]

What did this mean? The tribunal reasoned that, by 1939, the humanitarian rules included in the Regulations annexed to Hague Convention IV of 1907 (ratified by Germany in 1909) and the Geneva Conventions of 1929 (ratified by Germany in 1934) – both in force during World War II – had been recognized by all civilized nations,[32] meaning that these rules had by then long acquired the status of customary international law applicable to all States, whether or not they were parties to these conventions.[33] The tribunal thus argued that the Nazi crimes had breached customary international law existing at the material time (1939) and that, therefore, it had not violated the nonretroactivity principle in dealing with Nazi crimes. In short, it appealed to "international custom." The Nazi leaders knew – or should have known – that their crimes breached longstanding and generally accepted humanitarian rules. The applicability of the 1907 Hague Conventions and 1929 Geneva Conventions as customary international law in 1939–1945 meant that the temporal background against which to pass legal judgment on the Nazi criminals consisted not of six but of forty-six years (namely from 1899, when the first Hague Conventions were concluded, to 1945).

The tribunal's argument became known as the *Nuremberg clause*. It was reaffirmed by the UN General Assembly in 1946, in the UDHR, and in an Advisory Opinion of the International Court of Justice.[34] In 1950, the International Law

---

[29] IMT, Trial, 254.   [30] Ibid., 168–70.

[31] Ibid., 218, 223. See also Radbruch; Jaspers, 49–50; Kelsen 1945 and 1947; Meltzer. Kelsen and Meltzer also discuss the 1928 Kellogg-Briand Pact (Paris Pact), which prohibited war as an instrument of national policy. Ratified by Germany (and not repudiated by the Nazis), it became an important basis for the Nuremberg trials.

[32] IMT, Trial, 253–254.   [33] Fuller treatment of the argument in De Baets 2022, 1590–1593.

[34] Nuremberg Principles; UDHR, Art. 11.2; ICJ, Legality, §80.

Commission reformulated the clause as a principle: "The fact that internal law does not impose a penalty for an act which constitutes a crime under international law does not relieve the person who committed the act from responsibility under international law."[35] "International law" includes customary international law. The nonretroactivity principle and the Nuremberg principle would later be integrated into Article 15 ICCPR, which states that "No one shall be held guilty of any criminal offence ... which did not constitute a criminal offence, under national *or international law*, at the time when it was committed" and that an act or omission is criminal when, "at the time when it was committed, it was criminal according to the *general principles of law recognized by the community of nations.*"[36] International law – whether as treaty, custom, or general principles – is invoked here.

One of the early and crucial applications of international customary law can be found in what many have called the *humanity principle*. This principle was formulated most famously in the so-called *Martens clause*, which in its original wording in the preamble of the second Hague Convention on the laws and customs of war on land of 1899 read:

> Until a more complete code of the laws of war is issued, the High Contracting Parties think it right to declare that in cases not included in the Regulations adopted by them, populations and belligerents remain under the protection and empire of the principles of international law, as they result from the usages established between civilized nations, from the laws of humanity and the requirements of the public conscience.[37]

The Martens clause provided criteria to regulate all the problems that the second Hague Convention did not foresee. In metaphysical language reminiscent of natural law, it bridged morality and law by recommending custom ("usages"), humanity, and conscience as a moral and legal compass for all conduct in armed conflict not explicitly covered by the convention. The clause was repeated with minor variations in scores of international law instruments. In the decades between 1899 and 1939, the Martens clause gradually entered the domain of international customary law, a development confirmed by the International Court of Justice in 1996.[38] Vividly invoking custom, the Martens clause had become custom itself.

In a similar movement, international law has gradually developed a system of universally applicable peremptory norms (*jus cogens norms*) – norms which are so fundamental that no derogation from them is permitted.[39] These norms are

---

[35] ILC, "Principles," Principle 2, 374–375.
[36] ICCPR Art. 15, and, for its non-derogability, Art. 4(2). Italics added by author.
[37] Convention (II), preamble recital 9. Background in De Baets 2022, 1593–1594.
[38] ICJ, Legality, §§78, 84, 87. See also ICJ, Legal Consequences of the Construction, §89.
[39] VCLT, Arts. 53, 64; CCPR, General Comment 29, §11; ARSIWA, Arts. 26, 40–41, 50.1(d); ILC, Fragmentation, §§361–379.

obligations *erga omnes*,[40] that is, obligations owed to the international community as a whole. The most authoritative list of such *jus cogens* norms includes the prohibition to start a war of aggression, the basic rules of international humanitarian law (such as the Martens clause), the right of self-determination, and key prohibitions in international criminal law (the prohibition of atrocity crimes, racial discrimination and apartheid, slavery, and torture).[41] Many legal scholars believe that breaches of these most fundamental norms are subject to universal jurisdiction.

Future-oriented effects. Other rules and principles stretch the temporal scope forward. One such rule provides that when complainants die during a trial, their *heirs* are usually allowed to continue the case. In some jurisdictions, criminal charges can be brought on behalf of the deceased. If, however, domestic criminal codes do not mention any time bars, they enable descendants to sue in the name of their ancestors indefinitely, thus enhancing the risk of stifling debate about historical events.[42]

Among other forward-looking devices, the *imprescriptibility principle* stands out. The principle prohibits prescription (the setting of time bars) for the prosecution of atrocity crimes, implying that as long as perpetrators of such crimes live, they can be prosecuted, and that as long as victims of such crimes or their immediate descendants live, the crimes can be judicially investigated. The principle had to ripen for decades. The history of the imprescriptibility idea starts after 1945, when it gradually dawned that atrocity crimes should be exempt from time bars, not only because they were complicated and thus required lengthy investigation, but also because they constituted such an affront to its direct and indirect victims and to humanity at large that leaving them unpunished was not an option, not even long after the fact.[43]

Action was taken in the 1960s, and in 1968, a UN convention that explicitly blocked the pending prescription in 1970, after twenty-five years, of World War II crimes in many countries was approved.[44] It had less effect than expected.[45] One of the reasons lay in its Article 1, which stipulated that no time bars must apply for gross crimes "irrespective of the date of their commission." Many feared that this time clause would open or reopen investigation of atrocity crimes in the further past and violate the nonretroactivity principle. The doubts surrounding the 1968 convention only dissipated around 1998, when, after

---

[40] ARSIWA, Art. 48.1(b); ILC, Fragmentation, §§380–409.
[41] ILC, Peremptory Norms, Annex.   [42] De Baets 2009, 72–108.
[43] SRTJR, Report [Guarantees of non-recurrence], §48.
[44] See Convention on Non-Applicability, Art. 1. Background in De Baets 2022, 1595–1597.
[45] The convention was approved with fifty-eight votes against seven, with thirty-seven abstentions and twenty-five absentees. In October 2024, it had fifty-six State Parties.

some fierce discussions about the non-applicability of time bars to war crimes, it was agreed to insert the imprescriptibility principle into the Rome Statute of the International Criminal Court – for future atrocity crimes, not those of the past.[46] Meanwhile, imprescriptibility for atrocity crimes is increasingly accepted as a rule of customary international law (though there is no consensus yet).[47]

One important consequence of the application of the imprescriptibility principle is that suspects can be prosecuted long after the fact. At the condition that such trials respect their presumption of innocence and do not convert into "courts of history" in which those aged suspects are supposed to symbolize a past evil regime in its entirety, imprescriptibility responds to a deeply felt need. Imprescriptibility is also closer to the historian's approach than prescription. Indeed, historians possess the power to reopen "cold cases" at any time. However, two dangers that threaten both judges of atrocity trials and historians investigating past crimes are *anachronism*, defined as the impermissible transfer of contemporary concepts and values to the past, and *hindsight bias*, defined as the distorting influence that knowledge of the outcome of a past situation exerts on a present judgment about that situation. The longer ago a case took place, the more likely these risks are at play.

Some States, like Argentina, have found another avenue for judicial investigation into atrocity crimes of which most plaintiffs or defendants are no longer alive: the so-called *truth trials* (Juicios por la Verdad). For example, in 2022 such a truth trial opened in Chaco Province to investigate the 1924 Massacre of Napalpí, a case of genocide, with testimonies from a 114-year-old survivor, from three deceased massacre survivors of whom taped interviews had been preserved, from surviving relatives informed by oral traditions, and from several historians. The rationale for the trial was found in the principle that, as an atrocity crime, genocide was imprescriptible and its investigation necessary to fulfill the rights of the victims and their relatives to the truth, to reparation, and to non-recurrence. According to the judge, establishing the truth had a symbolic, historical, and human value. Acting as the plaintiff in the case, the Chaco governor said that the perpetrators "deserve[d] to be convicted in the collective memory of the indigenous peoples." The court found the State guilty of the genocide and ordered historical and symbolic reparations: The massacre was to be added to Argentina's school syllabus and forensic efforts to find the victims' remains had to continue.[48]

Like the imprescriptibility principle, the rules for *State succession* stretch the reach of human rights into the future. In the law of treaties, new States are *not* bound by treaties of predecessors because they experience a fundamental

---

[46] ICC, Rome Statute, Art. 29.   [47] See, e.g., "List of Customary Rules," Rule 160.
[48] Juzgado, 221–227.

change in circumstances (a doctrine known as *rebus sic stantibus*).[49] There is, however, consensus that when new States are established, the rule of continuity with the predecessor State still applies to one particular type of obligation: the humanitarian and human rights of their citizens.[50] The UN Human Rights Committee has explained the paramount reason for this:

> [T]he rights enshrined in the Covenant [the ICCPR] belong to the people living in the territory of the State party ... [O]nce the people are accorded the protection of the rights under the Covenant, such protection devolves with territory and continues to belong to them, notwithstanding change in government of the State party, including dismemberment in more than one State or State succession.[51]

Another principle that expands the time scope into the future is the *intertemporal law principle*. It was developed by Swiss Arbitrator Max Huber at the Permanent Court of Arbitration in 1928 while arbitrating in an inter-State dispute. Huber formulated the two-pronged principle as follows:

> [A] juridical fact must be appreciated in the light of the law contemporary with it and not of the law in force at the time when a dispute in regard to it arises or falls to be settled ... As regards the question which of different legal systems prevailing at successive periods is to be applied in a particular case (the so-called intertemporal law), a distinction must be made between the creation of rights and the existence of rights. The same principle which subjects the act creative of a right to the law in force at the time the right arises, demands that the existence of the right, in other words its continued manifestation, shall follow the conditions required by the evolution of law.[52]

The intertemporal principle refers to juridical facts. Many juridical facts are open-ended: For example, the search, identification, and protection of the war dead; the exhumation and criminal investigation of deaths or the return of human remains; and the maintenance of, and access to, gravesites are all long-term obligations of international humanitarian law. The principle means that the law contemporaneous with the juridical facts must prevail, implying that different legal regimes may be applicable to the same juridical facts at different times. If some juridical facts persist over time, their "continuing manifestation" implies that the law contemporaneous with them *is* the law at the time of the dispute.[53]

---

[49] VCLT, Art. 62; Vienna Convention on Succession, Arts. 8–9.

[50] VCLT, Arts. 38, 43, 73; Vienna Convention on Succession, preamble recital 6, Arts. 5, 31, 34–35. See also IACtHR, Velásquez Rodríguez, §184.

[51] CCPR, General Comment 26, §4; CCPR, General Comment 31, §15.

[52] ICA, Island of Palmas Case, 845. See also VCLT, Art. 31.3, and ICJ, Legal Consequences for States, §53. See also ILC, Fragmentation, §§475–478; Elias; Wheatley; Koskenniemi, 56–60.

[53] ARSIWA, Art. 13.

Past- and future-oriented effects. A factor with the capacity to expand the time horizon in both directions is the estimated *extension in time of wrongful acts*, a notion first introduced by Heinrich Triepel in 1899. Under the doctrine of State responsibility for internationally wrongful acts, wrongful acts can be instantaneous, continuing, or composite. An *instantaneous breach* occurs at the time of the State act or State omission, even if the effects of that breach continue or are lasting. A *continuing breach* extends over the entire period during which a State act or omission continues. A *composite breach*, finally, is a breach through a series of repetitive State acts or omissions defined in aggregate as a wrongful practice, pattern, or systematic policy.[54] If a continuing or composite breach started before the critical date and continued after it, the breach can only be adjudicated for the period after the critical date. This is without prejudice of customary international law and *jus cogens* norms which may, as we saw, be applicable regardless of the critical date and move the starting point of the breach backward.If a continuing breach is prescriptible, the limitation period starts only when the breach has ceased (and not when it arises).

Many gross human rights violations – such as enforced disappearances, sexual slavery, conscription of children, forcible population transfer, unlawful occupation, or the maintenance of colonial domination by force – extend over time and are therefore regarded as continuing breaches; large-scale atrocity crimes or a system such as apartheid are considered to be composite breaches.[55] This discussion of the time scale of different breaches is analogous to the discussions in historiography about aggregated facts and the scale and complexity of different historical events.

Internationally wrongful acts do not only possess a *substantive* element – the material breaches themselves – but also a *procedural* element. This procedural element consists in the State failure to annul the breaches through procedural measures, in the first place measures to stop them, to guarantee nonrepetition, and to investigate them.[56] The persistent procedural failure of a State to acknowledge and investigate gross breaches of human rights committed by its representatives is seen as a *separate* breach of Article 2.3 ICCPR (the right to an effective remedy).[57] If a State fails to investigate effectively a wrongful death or disappearance attributable to it, for example, it is responsible for two continuing breaches: the substantial breach of wrongful death or disappearance and the procedural breach of not investigating it effectively.

But what does "*effective investigation*" mean? Effectively investigating a breach of the past requires – as a minimum – that the State does not cleanse,

---

[54] Ibid., Arts. 14–15.   [55] Background in De Baets 2022, 1594–1595.   [56] ARSIWA, Art. 30.
[57] CCPR, General Comment 31, §§15–18.

close, or overclassify the relevant archival records; that it does not stretch, obstruct, or discontinue any ongoing procedure under the cover of secrecy or other false pretenses such as that the conduct did not constitute a criminal offense at the time, that the events were time-barred or subject to amnesty; and that it does not adopt an attitude of bureaucratic indifference toward requests of complainants or impose on them an unreasonable burden to prove their victim status or the truth of their allegations (especially for violations that occurred in secrecy and/or longer ago). In addition, basic evidentiary measures – autopsies and exhumations, for example – should be undertaken according to recognized protocols. The responsibility to investigate is also revived whenever compelling new evidence in a case emerges.

The State responsibility to investigate is a responsibility of means, not of result: Relatives of victims cannot *compel* governments to take particular actions. In addition, it does not include all the deaths of history ("the historical deaths") or all the cases of torture or disappearance that have not yet been investigated. The European Court of Human Rights, for example, has argued that the responsibility to investigate applies only to breaches for which a "genuine connection" with the critical date can be established or to breaches that fail to uphold fundamental humanitarian values. It has determined criteria for what constitutes a "genuine connection" and from when "fundamental values" play a role, but these criteria have raised many questions.[58] The discussion about how far back in time courts must go in adjudicating claims of ineffective investigation of past breaches is not yet satisfactorily resolved.[59]

Be that as it may, the International Court of Justice and other courts have frequently referred to the notion of continuing breaches.[60] It was inserted into the 1991 Draft Articles on Responsibility of States for Internationally Wrongful Acts and it will be part of a future Convention on Responsibility of States for Internationally Wrongful Acts. However, the notion was not taken up in the Rome Statute of the International Criminal Court.

2.3 The Passage of Time

Finally, there is one claim that can work in all directions: the passage of time. In discussing this claim, it is useful to distinguish events of longer ago from recent events. As a general rule, the passage of time dejudicializes events of longer ago. With the passage of time, crimes and other human rights violations

---

[58] Overviews of the discussion are provided in Moynihan; Schabas.

[59] Other jurisdictions have equally controversial critical dates: see, e.g., the discussion in Brazil about the "temporal landmark thesis" (or "time requirement principle").

[60] See CCPR, General Comment 31, §19; CCPR, General Comment 36, §27. A discussion of more recent cases is provided in Baranowska.

gradually slip out of reach of adjudication. As Jean-Denis Bredin distinctively put this point:

> Undoubtedly, in the course of time [the harm inflicted on the heir] softens. Modern law cherishes the nuclear family and is not interested in distant heirs. Widowers or widows, children, grandchildren, they are allowed to demand before court the price for their honor or suffering when their relative has been wronged. Beyond this, it is doubtful that the heir captures the judge's attention. Collateral distance, the passing of time, and the notoriety of persons or events make his intervention unlikely. Twentieth-century history should be on its guard against the law. The history of the French Revolution is almost without risk. Medieval history opens very quiet horizons. There comes a time when graves are no longer adorned with flowers, when the dead seem really dead. Then the law leaves the historian alone.[61]

Historians can investigate facts of longer ago without the threat of legal action. Even so, periods of longer ago – for example, periods of ethnogenesis or other formative events – can be very sensitive subjects.

For recent events – defined as events during which their protagonists are still alive – the situation is more complex because the public interest in knowing what happened, especially when atrocity crimes and wrongdoing are involved, has to be balanced against the interests of defendants in privacy and reputation and State interests in secrecy. In the case of defendants, the presumption in favor of disclosure of information about individuals who are public figures, in particular politicians, is strong and courts generally reckon with shorter deadlines if the latter file complaints to stop this information from being released.[62] When these politicians and other public figures are recently deceased, the presumption in favor of disclosure becomes even stronger.[63] In the State case, the presumption in favor of disclosure of information about atrocities and wrongdoing is overriding, whether or not the defendants are still alive.[64]

In short, the disclosure of information is greatly supported by passage of time claims for atrocity crimes and wrongdoing of longer ago and for those involving recently deceased individuals, and by a strong presumption in favor of disclosure for those involving still living public figures. The greater freedom of historical research that follows has a downside in the quantity and quality of available sources: For events of longer ago, the records risk being lost; for recent events, the records risk being distorted, destroyed, or not created at all.

---

[61] Bredin, 98 (author's translation).

[62] The ECtHR has understood the passage of time in this way (e.g., in Lehideux and Isorni, §55; Perinçek, §§249–250).

[63] For this presumption, see GDPR, Considerations 27, 158, 160.

[64] For this presumption, see Reparation Principles, Art. 24; Tshwane Principles, Principles 10A, 21(c).

2.4 Conclusion

Of all the previously discussed factors that influence the possibilities of judicial investigation over time, three are paramount: whether an event is recent or not, whether it is a crime or not, and whether their victims and perpetrators are alive or not. From a human rights perspective, the recent past – the time span of the generations who are living now – is of more concern than the remote past – the time span of past generations – although the latter is certainly not exempted from scrutiny. The human rights time regime oscillates. One set of principles and rules (e.g., nonretroactivity, *ratione temporis*, finality, prescription, amnesty) favors a time regime of relative immediacy, while another set of principles stretches the applicability of human rights over several generations.

Although the main perspective on time is linear in both the disciplines of law and history, the human rights view of time is different from the historian's view of time. The historian has shown a traditional preference to reason in terms of regimes of historicity for entire eras and to identify large episodes of continuity alternated by short episodes of change. Recently, philosophers of history have also explored ruptures in time and even temporal reversibility and anarchy. In contrast, the time scope of human rights is distilled from deeply held convictions about the relationship between time, crime, and justice. The principles they apply are the sediment of a profound and often age-old search to reconcile these three requirements.

If we remember that it is not international law's mission to develop a historical vocabulary or a consistent philosophy of time nor to judge macro-historical structures of injustice in the abstract, we must conclude that although the general time regime of law is one of *immediacy* and sits uneasily with historians looking at the long term, it stands under the strong influence of the *longue durée* precisely when applied to human rights issues. All in all, the time scope of human rights is governed by a *mixed time regime*. This time regime allows a rather broad horizon for dealing in earnest with a repressive and conflictive past – two generations (roughly seventy years), and occasionally three (roughly one century) – and constitutes the appropriate background for discussing the dimensions of memory and history in the next sections.

Intermezzo: The International Freedom of Expression Framework

A grasp of the international framework of freedom of expression is crucial if I want to analyze the human rights view of memory and history in the next sections. This normative framework, created by the United Nations, consists of Articles 19 and 20 ICCPR:

Article 19 ICCPR

1. Everyone shall have the right to hold opinions without interference.
2. Everyone shall have the right to freedom of expression; this right shall include freedom to seek, receive and impart information and ideas of all kinds, regardless of frontiers, either orally, in writing or in print, in the form of art, or through any other media of his choice.
3. The exercise of the rights provided for in paragraph 2 of this article carries with it special duties and responsibilities. It may therefore be subject to certain restrictions, but these shall only be such as are provided by law and are necessary:
   (a) For respect of the rights or reputations of others;
   (b) For the protection of national security or of public order (ordre public), or of public health or morals.

Article 20 ICCPR

1. Any propaganda for war shall be prohibited by law.
2. Any advocacy of national, racial or religious hatred that constitutes incitement to discrimination, hostility or violence shall be prohibited by law.

Both articles relate to opinions, but their paragraphs refer to specific states of these opinions: Article 19.1 to their *formation*, Article 19.2 to their *expression*, Article 19.3 to their *restriction*, and Article 20 to their *prohibition*. Articles 19 and 20 ICCPR are surrounded by Article 17 (the rights to privacy and reputation), Article 18 (the right to freedom of thought, conscience, and religion), Article 21 (the right to peaceful assembly), and Article 22 (the right to freedom of association), which will often be considered in conjunction.

Article 19.1 has an absolute character. The UN Human Rights Committee held that "[i]t is incompatible with paragraph 1 [of Article 19 ICCPR] to criminalize the holding of an opinion."[65] If a State restricts an opinion, it can never do so on the basis of its content alone; it should also consider the context in which the opinion is expressed. Article 19.1 should be understood in combination with Article 18.1, which reads: "Everyone shall have the right to freedom of thought, conscience and religion." Both articles refer to an individual's *forum internum*, the realm of one's conscience and inner thought. Individuals are free to develop, hold, adopt, and change thoughts and opinions without any coercion or interference: not only are these rights universal (they are applicable to everyone), but also, unlike most other human rights, absolute (they must never be restricted by the State) and non-derogable (they must be fully respected during public emergencies).[66] The *forum*

---

[65] CCPR, General Comment 34, §9.

[66] For the *forum internum*, see SRFRB, Report; for the dangers of interfering with it, SRFRB, Interim Report. See also Bublitz and Dresler.

externum, referring to the expression of thoughts and opinions in public, is the subject of Articles 19.2 and 19.3.

Article 19.2 defines the right to freedom of expression, subdivided in the right to search and access ("seek"), collect ("receive"), and disseminate ("impart") information and ideas.

Article 19.3 embodies the idea that while the right to freedom of expression is universal, its exercise in public is not absolute but subject to restrictions. Accordingly, Article 19.3 describes a test to assess the permissibility of restrictions. I will therefore call Article 19.3 *the permissible restrictions clause*. The first branch of the clause contains the *legality principle*: The restriction should be "provided by law," meaning that the law should stipulate the restriction, and be transparent (publicly accessible) and predictable (clear and precise). The second branch describes the *legitimacy principle*: It lists the legitimate interests on which restrictions can be based. These can be individual (the rights or reputations of others) or collective (national security, public order, public health, and public morals). Let us briefly comment on each interest.

- The "rights of others" can restrict one's free expression. One's human rights end where these of others begin. Pursuant to this restriction, rights such as the privacy (Article 17 ICCPR), the nondiscrimination (Article 26 ICCPR), or the copyright (Article 15.1(c) ICESCR) of others may restrict one's freedom of expression. Many memory-related issues, for example, fall within the ambit of the rights to privacy and reputation.
- The "reputations of others" restriction is mentioned separately. Reputation (Article 17 ICCPR) is an individual's good name. Laws that protect reputation – called defamation laws – shield individuals against false statements of fact that demonstrably harm their reputations. However, while the right to free expression includes a right to criticize, offend, shock, and disturb, there is no right to be free from criticism and ridicule or a right not to be offended.[67] Freedom of expression is a robust right that should not be silenced by empty allegations of insult or defamation or by threats to sue for defamation. Defamation laws only comply with human rights standards if they protect the actual reputations of living individuals; they are not justified if their purpose is to protect the "reputations" of abstract entities (e.g., States, nations, religions, symbols, doctrines), deceased persons, or officials who are criticized for wrongdoing.[68]

---

[67] SRFEX, Report [Hate speech], §§53, 78.

[68] Article 19, *Defining*, Principle 2. Along with abusive defamation laws, other law types such as insult laws, blasphemy laws, heresy laws, and *lèse majesté* laws are incompatible with human rights standards and should be repealed: see CCPR, General Comment 34, §§38, 48.

- "National security" should be understood as the protection of "the existence of the nation or its territorial integrity or political independence against force or threat of force."[69] This State interest includes the possibility to keep sensitive information secret. The information categories that are kept secret, however, are often construed too broadly, especially if they include embarrassing evidence on crimes, foreign policy, armed conflict, civil unrest, military and police operations, and the control of minorities.
- "Public order" is "the sum of rules which ensure the functioning of society or the set of fundamental principles on which society is founded."[70] Public order helps regulate protests, demonstrations, and other forms of freedom of expression and assembly.
- "Public health" refers to measures of prevention and care for dealing with serious threats to the health of the population.[71]
- "Public morals," while varying according to eras and cultures, refer to "the maintenance of respect for fundamental values of the community."[72] Restrictions in the name of morals may not violate the nondiscrimination principle, meaning that they must not favor one group over others.[73]

Significantly, this list of six interests is exhaustive. This means that restrictions in the name of custom, culture, community, fatherland, flag, memory, national pride, or tradition are not permissible.

The third branch of the clause describes the *necessity principle*. Any restriction should be "necessary" to achieve the protection of the permissible interest: It must address a pressing social need and be proportional. Restrictions that are "unnecessary" or "disproportional" (for example, harsh sanctions) produce effects that chill free expression.[74] In short, States should exercise self-restraint when restricting freedom of expression. The restrictions themselves are restricted. If States fail on any part of the permissible restrictions clause, they violate the right to freedom of expression.

Article 20 ICCPR, finally, describes propaganda for war – incitement to war (Article 20.1) – and hate speech – incitement to discrimination, hostility, or violence (Article 20.2). Its main message is that both types of incitement should be prohibited by law.[75] Opinions, however, should pass a high threshold before they can be called hate speech. The reason is that otherwise any critical opinion risks being dismissed as hate speech. One of the questions addressed here is whether the denial of past atrocity crimes is a form of hate speech.

---

[69] Siracusa Principles, §29.   [70] Ibid., §22.   [71] Ibid., §25.   [72] Ibid., §27.
[73] CCPR, General Comment 34, §32.   [74] Ibid., §§34–35.
[75] In addition, ICERD, Art. 4, stipulates that incitement to racial discrimination should be criminalized ("punishable by law").

This is, in a nutshell, the international freedom of expression framework. It will be our guide while discussing the human rights view of memory and history.

3 A Human Rights View of Memory

Embedded in time, our past-related ideas, emotions, and activities revolve around two poles: memory and history. In this section, I will explain what human rights have to say about memory.

3.1 Memory and the Dead

When we look back at past events and ruminate over them, we create memories. Memory is eminently related to the past, as when we think of family members and friends that we lost or of political and cultural leaders who died after they left their mark on our country for long periods, for example. Memories about dead persons are a paradigmatic case of memories in general. This is so because dead persons – and recently deceased persons in particular – are located at the point of transition from present to past. Dead persons belong to the past because they have died but they also belong to the present because after their deaths they continue to exist substantially (as human remains), genetically (in their offspring), narratively (in life stories), and symbolically (in the personal legacy and the tangible and intangible heritage they leave behind). Whether appearing in substantial, genetical, narrative, or symbolic shapes, whether evoked in emotional circumstances or used as evidence in arguments, dead persons arguably constitute a main portal to memory and, as such, to the past.

But from a human rights point of view, dead persons are problematic. Nobody will dispute that the living – as human beings – are entitled to human rights. Dead persons, however, are not alive anymore; hence, they are *not* human beings. Although they continue to live after their deaths in the ways distinguished above, they are *past* human beings. This primordial fact has four consequences. First, it means that the dead do not have human rights. Second, the fragile dignity that unmistakably characterizes the dead is not human dignity but another kind of dignity that can best be described as posthumous dignity. Third, the legal and moral wrongs to which the dead can be and are subjected are technically not human rights violations. Last but not least, the fact that the dead do not have human rights does not imply that the living do not have responsibilities to the dead; on the contrary, they have such responsibilities related to the bodies, property, and personalities of the dead.[76] This brief characterization of

---

[76] This thesis is developed in De Baets 2023b.

the ambiguous ontological status of dead persons is a necessary prelude for understanding the subtle relationship between human rights and memory.

3.2 Memory as a Right

The starting point of my human rights analysis of memory consists of a paradox: The ICCPR does not mention memory, and yet memory – the act of remembering – is a right that enjoys robust protection under it. How is that possible? The ICCPR recognizes the right to freedom of thought and the right to freedom of opinion (Articles 18.1 and 19.1 ICCPR). And memories are a type of thought and opinion. Therefore, everything that the ICCPR has to say about thoughts and opinions is applicable to memories. Let me explain this.

The view that memory is a type of thought is widely accepted: Thinking is a conscious or semi-conscious activity of the mind that can be directed toward the past, the present, or the future. When thought is directed toward the past, it often mobilizes declarative memory and produces memories.[77] This implies that although not all thoughts are memories, all memories are thoughts. In addition, thought and opinion are intimately related: The creation of thought – thinking – is a process; the result of that process is an opinion.[78] This connection entails that memories are not only types of thought, but, if they crystallize, also types of opinion. Therefore, ICCPR provisions about thought and opinion equally apply to memories. And if a right to freedom of thought and opinion exist, then a right to memory exists as well.

Two complaints before the UN Human Rights Committee may illustrate the right to memory. In 2009, while considering the case *Cifuentes* v. *Chile*, about a student who disappeared under the Pinochet dictatorship, two committee members observed:

> When the State has been responsible [for a disappearance], it is . . . unacceptable for it to fail to provide family members with the answers they need to be able to mourn, as is their right, disappeared persons who have been extrajudicially executed . . . If the person has died, family members must be allowed to exercise their right to mourn the person so that they may try to continue on as best as they can under such tragic circumstances, and the State should guarantee them that right.[79]

In *Schedko* v. *Belarus*, the complainant was not informed of the date, hour, or place of the execution of her son (who had been convicted of murder and

---

[77] Declarative memory is memory expressed in language – as opposed to habit or procedural memory.

[78] Hammer, 54, 61; Nowak, 441.

[79] CCPR, Cifuentes, dissenting opinion of Keller and Salvioli, §§12–31, especially 29, 31.

sentenced to death). In addition, the body was not returned for burial and the location of the grave was unknown to her. The committee commented: "The Committee considers that the authorities' initial failure to notify the author of the scheduled date for the execution of her son, and their subsequent persistent failure to notify her of the location of her son's grave amounts to inhuman treatment of the author, in violation of article 7 of the Covenant."[80] Alongside the fact that in both cases the committee criticized the State for procedural breaches (see Section 2), it also firmly defended the right to mourn, which is an important form of the right to memory. I conclude that the right to memory enjoys strong protection under human rights.

Memory as a right with restrictions. Memories can be located in the *forum internum* or the *forum externum*. The former enjoy absolute protection, the latter do not. Expressions of collective memory,[81] particularly public commemorations at funerals, in processions, and at demonstrations, should be protected by the rights to freedom of expression (Article 19.2 ICCPR) and peaceful assembly (Article 21 ICCPR), even if they upset others, and not banned. However, they may be restricted under the permissible restrictions clause. In between both *fora* lies a zone of transition: the zone where memories are expressed in the privacy of the home, for example, during periods of grief: This zone is protected by the right to privacy (Article 17 ICCPR) against arbitrary or unlawful interference and therefore the grounds for State restrictions on commemorations organized at home and within the family are virtually nonexistent.

One permissible restriction on the expression of memory is "the rights and reputations of others": Public commemorations should not intrude on the privacy of others or harm their reputations. Another permissible restriction is "public order": Processions, gatherings around monuments, and so on should occur peacefully. If they disturb the public peace, or when there is an imminent risk they will do, they may be policed. In addition, public commemorations can be temporarily suppressed in times of emergency. Restrictions on peaceful public commemorations, however, should satisfy the necessity principle: The measures taken should be proportional to the risks. In practice, the necessity principle is often violated because many commemorations are improperly suppressed or obstructed across the globe.

There is, however, one situation in which the restriction of commemorations is clearly justified: when they express reverence for dead tyrants and mass murderers and their crimes, and thus risk becoming triggering factors for new

---

[80] CCPR, Schedko, §10.2.
[81] The ICCPR ignores the concept of "collective memory" but protects its expression in collective commemoration.

violence. As the UN Office of the High Commissioner for Human Rights formulated it: "Commemoration events of past crimes or of traumatic or historical episodes … can exacerbate tensions between groups, including the glorification of perpetrators of atrocities."[82] States may permissibly restrict public commemorations likely to incite hatred and violence on the grounds of the rights of others or public order under Article 19.3 ICCPR or prohibit the worst cases altogether under Article 20.2 ICCPR.

3.3 Memory as a Responsibility

Another question that arises is whether memory constitutes a responsibility. Here I should distinguish two situations: memory as a right with responsibilities and memory as a responsibility rather than a right. I will discuss them successively for individuals and for States.

Memory as a right with individual responsibilities. Forming and holding memories, as *forum internum* rights, do not come with any responsibilities. Nor does the expression of memories in private. Expressing memories in public, as a *forum externum* right, however, is different. According to Article 19.3 ICCPR, the right to freedom of expression comes with "special duties and responsibilities." In the case of commemorating dead persons in public, two such responsibilities can be distinguished: a responsibility to respect the dead and a responsibility to protect them. What does this mean?

All of the living maintain thick relations with the few dead whom they admired and loved (their dead relatives, perhaps their deceased best friends) and thin relations with the many dead whom they did not know. To the former they hold an individual *responsibility to protect* to varying degrees (for example, to tend their graves or urns); to the latter they hold a general *responsibility to respect.* The responsibility to protect those with whom we have thin relations is taken care of either by others or collectively, including by the State. If the responsibilities of respect and protection are met in decent ways, we can speak of a *responsible memory.*[83]

Memory as a right with State responsibilities. According to the ICCPR, States have responsibilities to respect, protect, and promote the right to memory of their citizens. A State *responsibility to respect* refers to the vertical relations between the State and its citizens. It means that the State, if it interferes with expressions of memory by its citizens, especially their expressions of grief, must strictly follow the permissible restrictions clause. A State *responsibility*

---

[82] OGPRP, Framework, 17.

[83] For another approach to the right to memory (often lacking in conceptual clarity, in my opinion), see Tirosh and Reading (eds.). For work on the politics of memory, see, among many others, Mälksoo (ed.), and Gutman and Wüstenberg (eds.).

to protect refers to the horizontal relations between its citizens. It means that the State must protect the expression of memory by its citizens and stop individuals or groups from unduly interfering with the expression of memory of others. This responsibility extends to the protection of peaceful unofficial commemorations, including those in opposition to official remembrance policies and those that upset others.[84] In addition, the State responsibility to protect is also a responsibility to protect the dead themselves and it is fulfilled if due care is taken of cemeteries, memorials, collective funerary rituals, archives, museums, and so on.[85]

A State *responsibility to promote*, finally, means that the State should facilitate the expression of memory by its citizens. Under this responsibility, States should promulgate effective and equitable public order laws and conduct official remembrance policies. They can find inspiration for these policies in the UN Reparation Principles, which explain that reparations for past human rights violations typically include measures of restitution, compensation, rehabilitation, satisfaction (or symbolic reparation), and nonrecurrence for survivors of such atrocities.[86] But how should States deal with the dead under their responsibility to promote? Four of the five reparation measures just mentioned come too late for those who died in past atrocities. What is left for them are measures of symbolic reparation, such as ascertaining and acknowledging the facts of past human rights violations; making or facilitating public apologies for past crimes committed by the State, its predecessor, or non-State agents; establishing anniversaries and memory sites; and ensuring that forgotten atrocity crimes are treated in history textbooks (as in the example of the Argentinian truth trial). Of course, families and non-State actors will also be active in the area of remembrance: The State should allow and assist – not restrict, boycott, or punish – these initiatives.

Memory as an individual responsibility rather than a right. I will now look into the second situation. When victims of past atrocities are commemorated, some critics do not merely see memory as a right that comes with responsibilities. They argue that the historical injustice afflicted to victims of past atrocities when they were alive should not continue after their deaths and that the dead should not die twice. In short, they defend the position that memory is less a right than an ineluctable responsibility itself. How does the ICCPR approach this claim? Individuals can *impose* a responsibility to remember dead persons such as victims of past atrocities *upon themselves*. Such a self-imposed moral duty is nothing else than an expansion of their right to remember. In contrast, any responsibility to remember *imposed on others* carries high risks of coercion

---

[84] See also SRFPAA, Joint Report, §§37–49; SRFPAA, Ten Principles, Principle 4.
[85] De Baets 2023b.   [86] Reparation Principles, §§19–23.

and manipulation if those imposing the responsibility possess political or other power and make biased selections of whom to remember and whom to forget. From a human rights perspective, the responsibility to remember imposed on others should be rejected.

Memory as a State responsibility rather than a right. Invoking their responsibility to promote, States have increasingly adopted so-called *memory laws*, which are of two types: declaratory memory laws that merely state that a certain historical fact is officially recognized and coercive memory laws that prescribe or proscribe certain views of the past regarding historical figures, symbols, dates, or events. From a human rights perspective, the declaratory type is allowed; the coercive type should be rejected. This is so because coercive memory laws either make certain historical views mandatory or prohibit other historical views. They create official narratives of the past interspersed with dogmas and taboos. In so doing, they generate significant chilling effects on the free expression of their citizens during commemorations and in historical research.

This means that the State responsibility to promote the right to memory does *not* include the promulgation of coercive memory laws. Such laws should be repealed because they do not satisfy the necessity principle: Mandatory official memories or histories are not "necessary" for or "proportional" to any of the interests mentioned in the permissible restrictions clause. In the words of the UN Human Rights Committee: "Laws that penalize the expression of opinions about historical facts are incompatible with the obligations that the Covenant imposes on States parties."[87] While requiring the prohibition of (historical) hate speech under Article 20.2 ICCPR and allowing punishment for it, the committee rejected coercive memory laws.

The noncoercion principle. The tendency of some individuals to impose memory as a responsibility on others and of States to enact coercive memory laws for society at large raises the question whether it is ever permitted to make memories mandatory. The answer is negative. Article 18.2 ICCPR, referring to the freedom of belief, among others, includes a fundamental noncoercion principle:

> No one shall be subject to coercion which would impair his freedom to have or to adopt a . . . belief of his choice.

---

[87] General Comment 34, §49, with a footnote clarifying that these laws are called "memory-laws." See also the *travaux préparatoires* in CCPR, 102nd Session, §§63–79, especially §68. The leading CCPR case concerning memory laws is CCPR, Faurisson (1996), a case of Holocaust denial in which France's Loi Gayssot was criticized. For commentary on the CCPR approach, see O'Flaherty 2012a, 652–653; de Zayas and Roldán Martín, 443–448; and more generally SAPG, Combating, 7–8. See also De Baets 2018, 47–55; Bán and Belavusau.

The UN Human Rights Committee has applied this principle to the freedoms of opinion and expression:

> Any form of effort to coerce the holding or not holding of any opinion is prohibited. Freedom to express one's opinion necessarily includes freedom not to express one's opinion.[88]

There is a right not to speak and a right to silence. This noncoercion principle is so important because the right to express opinions is seriously undermined if it compels individuals to express opinions that they do not hold in honesty or that they feel are premature. Application of the noncoercion principle is key to understanding memory in relation to responsibility: It means that nobody can be compelled to express memories or comply with a responsibility to remember past events imposed on them by others or by the State. In other words, there is no such thing as a right to be remembered.

Yet, although States must not *coerce* their citizens to adopt certain opinions about the past, under their responsibility to promote they should *balance* their powers to promote official memories – in the name of public morals or the rights and reputations of others – against the freedom of expression and the right to silence of their citizens. Such a balancing act will define the role of States when they act as speakers, educators, or funders in the realm of memory.[89] It will decide the extent to which attendance of official commemorations is obligatory (highly likely for members of the political and military apparatus, much less so for others), the extent to which the history outlined in school curricula and textbooks should be mandatorily taught in the classroom and become subject of exams, even against the wish of protesting parents, and the extent to which non-State organizations are funded for remembrance activities. The balancing act of the State may legitimately restrict freedom of expression and result in some responsibilities of compliance for selected categories of citizens.

3.4 Forgetting as a Right

The noncoercion principle also raises two new questions: Is there a right to forget and is there a right to be forgotten? The answer is affirmative twice, but with important nuances.

The right to forget. Strictly speaking, *no* right to forget exists in the human rights vocabulary. However, the noncoercion principle tells us that nobody can be

---

[88] CCPR, General Comment 22, §§5, 8; CCPR, General Comment 34, §10. See also SRFRB, Report, §34. For the notions of "thought," "belief," and "coercion" in the ICCPR *travaux préparatoires*, see Hammer, 49–68 (for Art. 18 ICCPR) and Aswad, 331–353 (for Art. 19.1 ICCPR).

[89] See also Brettschneider, 1–23.

compelled to express memories. Therefore, the right to forget amounts to the right not to be forced to remember (including to mourn or commemorate) against an individual's will. The right to forget is absolute in the *forum internum*, but it can be restricted in the *forum externum*: While it is always prohibited to force memories upon others and thereby expel their wish for oblivion, the expression of the right to forget can be restricted. If the "rights of others" is a permissible restriction for one's free expression, it also is for one's freedom not to express opinions. While individuals wishing to publicly commemorate are required to *balance* their wish with the privacy and reputation of those refusing to remember or wishing to forget, individuals wishing to forget, in turn, should remember three rules of the thumb. First, they have no right to deny others to commemorate privately or in public. Second, a right to forget is not the same as an (often preached) *responsibility to forget*: It is not possible to impose forgetting, either on others or on oneself – although amnesties (discussed in Section 2) may lead to legal and eventually to social forgetting. Finally, the right to forget should not degenerate into a denial that certain events, including atrocities, have taken place in the past. For example, neo-Nazi parents cannot invoke a right to forget to justify nonattendance of history lessons on the Holocaust by their children.

The right to be forgotten. The next question is whether one has a right to control what others are allowed to know about oneself. This right to forget one's own past – known as the right to erasure or the right to be forgotten – is a radical form of the right to privacy (Article 17 ICCPR), and privacy is a permissible restriction of freedom of expression.

The UN Human Rights Committee maintained that:

> [E]very individual should have the right to ascertain in an intelligible form, whether, and if so, what personal data is stored in automatic data files, and for what purposes. Every individual should also be able to ascertain which public authorities or private individuals or bodies control or may control his or her files. If such files contain incorrect personal data or have been collected or processed contrary to the provisions of the law, every individual should have the right to have his or her records rectified.[90]

Individuals (should) have a right to rectification of incorrect personal data held on them but no right to erase them. At the global level, a right to be forgotten does not exist. Although this is a worldwide issue, it has been most intensely discussed in Europe. In 2014, the Court of Justice of the European Union recognized a right to be forgotten which was to be activated when the processed personal data were "inadequate, irrelevant or no longer relevant,

---

[90] CCPR, General Comment 34, §18; also CCPR, General Comment 16, §10.

or excessive in relation to those purposes and in the light of the time that has elapsed."[91] Following this line, the European Union's General Data Protection Regulation, entered into force in 2016, provides for the right to have publicly available personal data erased when they are "no longer necessary" in relation to the purposes for which they were processed.[92]

A person seeking the right to be forgotten has to be alive, however: The Regulation does not apply to personal data of deceased persons.[93] In addition, the right to be forgotten does not apply to the processing of personal data for archiving, scientific, statistical, or historical (including genealogical) research purposes.[94] These purposes explicitly include the processing of personal data for research into one's political behavior under former totalitarian States or into atrocity crimes, in particular the Holocaust.[95] As argued in Section 2, the presumption in favor of disclosure of information is overriding in the cases of deceased persons and atrocity crimes.

The right to be forgotten has been invoked, with some success, by certain categories of individuals, for example former criminals who want to resume their life after a spent conviction and therefore demand erasure of their former convictions in the easily retrievable internet archives of news outlets. This application of the right to be forgotten, however, seriously jeopardizes the integrity of the content of internet archives and therefore judges have been inclined to prefer a right of reply or, somewhat stronger, an obligation for platforms to delink the problematic information from their search engines.

3.5 Memory and Tradition versus History

Memory, tradition, and history are three different ways to look at and cope with the past. Sometimes they operate in unison, often they operate independently, and sometimes they conflict. When historians formulate facts and opinions about dead persons that are contested in court, judges will look at whether these utterances can be permissibly restricted. Among the permissible restrictions are the privacy and reputations of the surviving relatives of the dead (and perhaps of the dead themselves) and society's public morals, but *not* memory or tradition.[96] Does this mean that the free expression about history can never be restricted in the name of memory and tradition? The answer is negative.

---

[91] CJEU, §93.   [92] GDPR, Art. 17.

[93] Ibid., Considerations 27, 158, 160. Analysis in De Baets 2016.

[94] GDPR, Art. 17.3(d); also Consideration 26, Arts. 5.1(e), 89.1. Data minimization, including pseudonymization, is recommended, however.

[95] Ibid., Considerations 73, 158.

[96] I define tradition, a form of memory, as a set of old customs and practices transferred over the generations and repeated in the present.

When does an appeal to respect the memory of the dead permissibly restrict free expression about history? The answer is that alleged attacks on that memory can be *reframed* as a permissible restriction, namely as an attack on "the rights or reputations of others." If so, historians can be sued because they supposedly showed no "respect for the memory of the dead," which under the reframing means that they have either attacked the privacy and reputation of the dead or of their surviving relatives. Courts are reluctant to consider the first possibility – posthumous privacy invasion and defamation – for a reason already stated: Dead persons do not have human rights such as the rights to privacy and reputation. In Section 2, I noted that, for similar reasons, the dead rarely receive legal victim status. Courts strongly prefer the second possibility, namely that the alleged posthumous defamation by the historian violated the rights to privacy and reputation of the surviving relatives. According to Article 17.2 ICCPR, everyone has the right to be protected by laws against privacy invasion and defamation. If relatives can demonstrate that certain opinions of historians about the dead defamed them *personally* or that the pain caused by these opinions invaded their *own* privacy, they have a substantial defense in court.

Likewise, when does an appeal to respect the tradition of ancestors permissibly restrict free expression about history? The answer is that alleged attacks on that tradition can be *reframed* as a permissible restriction, namely as "an attack on public morals." If so, historians can be sued because they supposedly showed no "respect for the tradition of the ancestors," which under the reframing means that they have either attacked the fundamental values of the community or its morals. Such a claim is acceptable in court if it can be demonstrated that community values and morals were effectively endangered by this disrespect of tradition and that these "community values" were not discriminatory, that is, were not in reality the exclusive values of a single privileged social group.[97]

If the evidence is convincing, a judge may see the "memory claim" – the distress caused by a historian's disrespect for the dead – as a violation of the relatives' privacy and reputation, and the "tradition claim" – the historian's disparagement of traditions to the extent that community values were genuinely undermined – as a breach of public morals. Within these strict limits, memory and tradition are acceptable checks on how historians deal with the past. Memory and tradition then trump history.

However, too much reverence for memory and tradition – let alone their sacralization – chills the freedom of expression of those who are critical toward

---

[97] Siracusa Principles, §§27–28; CCPR, General Comment 22, §8; CCPR, General Comment 28, §5; CCPR, General Comment 34, §§24, 32; CESCR, General Comment 21, §19; O'Flaherty 2012b, 348–349. For the UN debate on tradition, see note 3.

these memories and traditions and may even make historical research impossible. In all these cases – the large majority – the memory of the dead and the tradition of the ancestors are problematic restrictions upon the writing and telling of history: In overprotecting them, memory and tradition distort and censor debates about the past. Memory and tradition then trample history.

3.6 Breaches of the Right to Memory

Denial of atrocity crimes. The preceding discussion shows that bold opinions about the past do not usually breach the right to memory. There is one exception, however: the denial of atrocity crimes. It is utterly disturbing that *all* atrocity crimes – not just genocides, but also crimes against humanity and war crimes – have their deniers. Those who allege that a given genocide or other atrocity crime did not occur or, if it did, does not qualify as an atrocity crime, even in the face of massive, corroborated evidence to the contrary, actually argue that the dead victims, if they died at all, did not die in such an atrocity and therefore do not deserve to be commemorated, and that the surviving victims lie about this and thus falsify history. Such denial is extremely painful and intensely defamatory. Moreover, it is often accompanied by the glorification of the perpetrators of these atrocity crimes.

If persistent, denial has the potential to incite hatred toward the victim groups and threaten their safety. Incitement to discrimination, hostility, or violence – hate speech for short – must be prohibited by law (Article 20.2 ICCPR).[98] Even worse, when the denial of atrocity crimes occurs in a context of mounting political tension and armed conflict, this rhetoric can become dehumanizing war propaganda (prohibited under Article 20.1 ICCPR),[99] persecution as a crime against humanity (punishable under the Rome Statute of the International Criminal Court), or direct and public incitement to genocide (punishable under the Genocide Convention and the Rome Statute).[100]

From a human rights perspective, laws prohibiting hate speech laws are obligatory, whereas laws prohibiting genocide denial are not: In fact, the latter are often superfluous. Either genocide denial crosses the threshold of hate speech or not.[101] If the threshold is crossed, genocide denial laws are superfluous because generic hate speech laws already prohibit genocide denial. If the

---

[98] See also CCPR, General Comment 11, §§1–2; OHCHR, Rabat Plan, §§14–19, 22; SAPG, Combating, 3, 6–7; ECtHR, Guide, §§191–210; UNESCO, History under Attack.

[99] The war crimes of intentional destruction of cultural heritage and outrages upon the dignity of the dead (i.e., mutilation of corpses and desecration of gravesites) are simultaneously breaches of the right to memory. See, e.g., "List of Customary Rules," Rules 38–40, 112–116.

[100] Genocide Convention, Art. III(c).

[101] See also SRFEX, Report [Hate speech], §44(c); O'Flaherty 2012a, 638; Parisi, 42–46, 52–53.

denial does not meet that threshold and thus cannot be banned, it can still be dealt with under the permissible restrictions clause as unduly interfering with "public order" (if it jeopardizes the safety of the survivor community) or "the rights or reputations of others" (if it invades the privacy or defames the reputations of the members of that community). The additional value of genocide denial laws is largely symbolic: They set a standard of civility by which a society signals that genocide denial transgresses that standard.

3.7 Conclusion

Human rights strongly protect the faculty and activity of memory, but its expression in public comes with some restrictions and responsibilities. The tentative conclusion of my analysis is that the right to memory – especially the right to remember the dead – would seem to have two functions. The first is intrinsic: The living can satisfy a deeply felt need to honor their beloved dead, including through rituals and symbolic measures. The second is instrumental: A responsible memory allows the expression of a rich diversity of thoughts and opinions about the dead, which contributes to the debate about history and therefore to the formation of historical awareness. The instrumental function, however, forms an arena of social and political struggle, making it vulnerable to manipulation and distortion. Therefore, all coercion in the field of memories should be rejected; only some carefully substantiated restrictions on their expression are legitimate.

4 A Human Rights View of History

History is different from memory. It is an evidence-based approach to the past that involves a scholarly community of practitioners – the historians – who follow certain critical methods and whose results are constantly evaluated within that community. In this sense, history is a description of past events ("facts") and a systematic reflection on that description ("opinions"). From a human rights perspective, this distinction is crucial.

4.1 Facts and Opinions

In the ICCPR, the term "fact" appears twice and the term "opinion" three times. However, the use of these two terms is somewhat obscured, as in crucial places they are replaced by synonymous terms. The key passage in Article 19.2 ICCPR states: "Everyone shall have the right to freedom of expression; this right shall include freedom to seek, receive and impart information and ideas of all kinds." "Information" refers to "facts," and "ideas" to "opinions."[102]

---

[102] For the distinction, see, e.g., Nowak, 305–306, 339.

Statements of opinion enjoy higher protection in the human rights framework than statements of fact in the sense that facts should be as accurate as possible, whereas opinions may vary widely (though not indefinitely). Most notably, the list of human rights includes a "freedom of opinion" but not a "freedom of fact." This human rights epistemology echoes journalist C. P. Scott's famous adage from 1921: "Comment is free, but facts are sacred." This is so because international courts perceive opinions, in contrast to facts, as not susceptible to a truth/falsity proof. In other words, statements of fact are amenable to verification tests that with strong probability prove their truth or falsity, while statements of historical opinion can only be subjected to plausibility tests.[103] The same verified set of facts can generate several plausible interpretations because historians weigh the set differently according to their values, affiliations, and world views.[104] In turn, unless they are intended as literary or artistic, opinions cannot be based entirely on fantasy; they should have a minimum factual foundation.[105] Legal scholar Robert Post has aptly summarized the debate about the fact–opinion distinction:

> Statements of fact make claims about an independent world, the validity of which [is] in theory determinable without reference to the standards of any given community, and about which we therefore have a right to expect ultimate convergence or consensus. Statements of opinions ... make claims about an independent world, the validity of which depends upon the standards or conventions of a particular community, and about which we therefore cannot expect convergence under conditions of cultural heterogeneity.[106]

The difference between facts and opinions, while often clear, is sometimes hard to make in practice. The determination of facts is always informed by one's value judgments and world views (which as interpretations are forms of opinions themselves) and hence by the authority of those who formulate these facts, even if the influence of the latter is kept in check by their community of peers and even if the part of interpretation in simple facts (on which consensus is easier to reach) is smaller than for aggregated facts. In turn, opinions can be difficult to assess because at one end of the spectrum some masquerade as facts, while at the other some are not based on facts at all. In cases where it is unclear whether a given statement is a fact or an opinion, international courts should err on the side of opinion (and thus assume higher protection levels). Although the human rights perspective sheds little light on the share of opinions in facts and the share of facts in opinions, the fact–opinion distinction is as important for human rights scholars as it is for historians.[107]

---

[103] CCPR, General Comment 34, §47; Mendel, Emilio Palacio, §§42–50. See also Post, 153–163, 388–392.

[104] Tucker, 8.   [105] See also Frankfurt, 28–31, 67.   [106] Post, 162.

[107] Controversially, the ECtHR has assigned the status of "established historical fact" to the Holocaust but not to other corroborated genocides, at the risk of creating a hierarchy among

4.2 Statements of Fact

In the ICCPR definition of freedom of expression just mentioned, "information" is used as a proxy for "facts," and therefore the search, collection, and dissemination of facts is protected by human rights. As regards the search and collection of facts, we already saw in Section 3 that the right to access information about one's personal data is strong. As regards the search and collection of information held by public authorities, personal or not, the UN Human Rights Committee observed: "Article 19, paragraph 2 embraces a right of access to information held by public bodies. Such information includes records held by a public body, regardless of the form in which the information is stored, its source and the date of production."[108] This access to official information should be regulated in effective right to information laws (also called freedom of information laws or access to information laws) and "based on the principle of maximum disclosure, establishing a presumption that all information is accessible subject only to a narrow system of exceptions."[109] Among the obvious requesters of such information are historians, for whom the availability of information is their raw material. The formula "regardless of . . . the date of production" is notable because it also refers to laws regulating public archives.

Indeed, the corollary of the right to information is that under their responsibility to promote, States should comply with two specific tasks. The first is a responsibility to promulgate effective archives laws. As the International Council on Archives stated: "[Archives] play an essential role in the development of societies by safeguarding and contributing to individual and community memory. Open access to archives enriches our knowledge of human society, promotes democracy, protects citizens' rights and enhances the quality of life."[110] Public records should be preserved and made accessible according to clear and fair conditions and within reasonable terms. This is the general rule, but in a human rights context it is specifically applicable to so-called repression archives, archives that contain records and traces of human rights violations, often located in ministries or military, paramilitary, security, or police bodies.[111] For such archives, the default presumption – already stated in Section 2 – should be in favor of disclosure (subject to reasonable restrictions to guarantee the privacy of victims described in them).[112]

---

genocides. See ECtHR, Cultural Rights, §§85–88. See also ECtHR, Factsheet, 2, 21; ECtHR, Perinçek, §§209–220.

[108] CCPR, General Comment 34, §18.

[109] IMFE, Joint Declaration [Access to information], 2.

[110] International Council on Archives, Preamble. See also ECtHR, Suprun.

[111] Impunity Principles, Principles 14–18, relate to "preservation of and access to archives bearing witness to violations."

[112] Ibid., Principle 15. See also ECtHR, Suprun.

A strong national archival system is a prerequisite for the second State responsibility, the responsibility to effectively investigate and prosecute past atrocities and report the findings. In Section 2, I discussed this procedural State responsibility. Evidently, investigating human rights breaches requires meticulous corroboration of facts. This fact-centeredness serves three purposes: It helps guarantee a fair trial for suspects, it has a reparatory effect on surviving victims, and it rebuts attempts to remain silent or lie about the breaches or conceal and deny them.

Roughly between 1990 and 2005 the UN Commission on Human Rights developed the so-called Impunity Principles as a strategy to investigate atrocities and fight the impunity of their perpetrators. Fact-finding is central to it. Principles 2–5 establish a "right to know":

> Every people has the inalienable right to know the truth about past events concerning the perpetration of heinous crimes and about the circumstances and reasons that led, through massive or systematic violations, to the perpetration of those crimes ... Societies ... may benefit ... from the creation of a truth commission ... to establish the facts surrounding those violations so that the truth may be ascertained and to prevent the disappearance of evidence.[113]

This right to know is also called "the right to the truth" in the preamble and Principle 2 of the Impunity Principles, and the latter expression has become common now. The right to the truth means that in dealing with past atrocities, families of victims but also society at large have a right to know the facts about past crimes so that vital parts of the life stories of victims and general patterns of repression can be reconstructed. The right to the truth is also necessary to claim rights of commemoration and reparation.

A famous case may illustrate the stakes. In a landmark decision of 1999, the Inter-American Commission on Human Rights made the Argentine government pledge to acknowledge the right to the truth of relatives of two disappeared individuals. In the case at hand, petitioner Carmen Aguiar de Lapacó had in vain sought access to military and civilian archives to trace her daughter, Alejandra Lapacó, an anthropology student, and Marcelo Butti, a history student, who had disappeared in 1977 under the military dictatorship. The government reached a friendly settlement with the petitioner, acknowledging that Aguiar had a right to the truth, including a "need" to mourn, not subject to prescription.[114]

---

[113] Impunity Principles, Principles 2, 5.

[114] IACHR, Aguiar de Lapacó (1999), §§2, 15 and (2000), §§2, 17.1. The case was initiated in the context of the so-called truth trials (see Section 2.2).

Cases like this reveal that two different types of human rights violations are at stake here. First, there is the violation of the rights of the victims themselves (in the Lapacó case, the right to life, among others). And then there is the violation of the rights of the families of these victims. This second type arises because the procedural failure of the State to effectively investigate the first type causes mental torture in the surviving families for the rest of their lives because they do not know what happened. Not knowing existential facts – dates of disappearances and deaths, reasons for killings – is a form of inhuman treatment and torture itself. This reasoning, linking State responsibility (the failure to investigate) with a human rights violation (the right not to be tortured) via an epistemological feature (the continuing ignorance of families), was a revolutionary step in thinking about suffering. It first appeared, as far as I know, in the case of *Quinteros* v. *Uruguay* before the UN Human Rights Committee in 1990, and was then repeated countless times, including in *Schedko* v. *Belarus* (quoted in Section 2).[115]

Most legal experts see the right to the truth as a procedural combination of the rights to an effective remedy, to information and to be free from inhuman treatment (Articles 2.3, 19.2, and 7 ICCPR, respectively).[116] It is so strong that neither an amnesty nor a change of government nor the passage of time (particularly the deaths of perpetrators and victims) can affect it (although they can complicate it). Many legal scholars think that meanwhile the right to the truth has gained the status of customary international law, meaning that all States should respect it regardless of whether they are parties to the ICCPR.

With its emphasis on establishing and corroborating historical facts for the benefit of society at large, the right to the truth is an indispensable first step in the search for broader historical truth, that is, an understanding of the life stories of the victims and the causes, development, and consequences of repressive patterns and structures of violence which made possible the atrocities inflicted on them. Such a fact-oriented emphasis, however, should not confuse fact-finding with historical writing itself; it is only a necessary step toward a historical interpretation.

Provided then that we do not forget that the right to the truth understood as a collective right is only a first step for understanding the past, we can call it "a right to history." Together with the "right to memory," the "right to history" is an important tool to cope with past events. This means that during the last decades, international human rights law has encouraged a certain rehabilitation of the notion of historical fact under the guise of a right to the truth. Nowhere clearer

---

[115] CCPR, Quinteros, §14; CCPR, F.A.J. and B.M.R.A, §§3.7, 7.6.
[116] OHCHR, Study (2006), §§41–46, 56–57; OHCHR, Study (2007), §§19–39, 83, 85.

than in the study of past atrocities do we see the importance of historical facts that are not distorted, denied, or censored. Many historians, however, have barely noticed this new development as they were too busy lamenting the crisis of historical truth in their own profession.[117]

4.3 Statements of Opinion

International human rights law does not require a proof of truth for opinions. Opinions are perceived as comments and value judgments not susceptible to proof. Accordingly, statements of opinion enjoy greater protection under human rights than statements of facts. When confronted with conflicts about history, international courts have reiterated time and again that freedom of expression includes the right of everyone to seek historical truth through inquiry and open debate and the right to express and exchange critical opinions on history – and on memory, tradition, and heritage, for that matter.[118] Citizens from all walks of life have an interest to search, access, collect, and disseminate historical information and ideas, and to participate in free and critical historical debate. Likewise, society at large has a strong collective interest in a robust public debate about history in its entirety because the historical truths that are its outcome may clarify the past, especially its dark episodes, *and* are instrumental in achieving other goals, such as creating a well-founded collective identity or strengthening democracy.

The concept of "ideas" used in Article 19.2 ICCPR refers to opinions, including opinions of a historical nature. The UN Human Rights Committee explained: "All forms of opinion are protected, including opinions of a political, scientific, historic, moral or religious nature."[119] "Opinions of a historic nature," then, encompass three types: memories; interpretations of historical events; and explicit moral judgments about the conduct of historical figures. Memories were discussed in Section 3. Let us now look at the two other types.

Interpretation of historical events and the right to err principle. One preliminary problem in interpreting the past is the question of the *retroactive applicability of modern legal concepts* (such as genocide) onto crimes of the past. In principle, this discussion is not difficult: Historians apply contemporary concepts to past events all the time. Evidently, they know how these past events were labeled at the material time but often prefer new and more precise concepts to describe them. Even if the label "genocide" is relatively recent (it was coined in 1944), the conduct covered by this crime – specified in Article 2 Genocide

---

[117] An overview of the discussion in the historical profession is provided in Jay, whose views on historical truth (and his defense of institutional justificationism) approximate those defended here from a human rights perspective.

[118] ECtHR, Cultural Rights, §§85–88.   [119] CCPR, General Comment 34, §9.

Convention – is not. Therefore, prudent and reasoned use of such concepts for past crimes is possible without running the risk of anachronism.

Regarding the act of interpreting historical events itself, the leading human rights principle is that everyone has a *right to err*, that is, a right to hold ideas which appear to be unfounded in the end. In the words of the UN Human Rights Committee, "The Covenant does not permit general prohibition of expressions of an erroneous opinion or an incorrect interpretation of past events."[120] Blanket bans on the dissemination of false ideas about past events are incompatible with human rights. False ideas can only be restricted if they were expressed with an intent to harm one of the interests mentioned in Article 19.3 ICCPR or prohibited if they incite war propaganda, discrimination, hostility or violence mentioned in Article 20 ICCPR.

The right to err is applicable to everyone. It is also indispensable to practice historical writing: Indeed, even after peer review some of the facts proposed by historians prove to be falsehoods and some of their opinions – that is, their interpretations and judgments – prove to be implausible. When the falsehoods or implausible theories are the result of sloppy work, historians can (and will) be blamed from an academic or professional point of view but not from a human rights point of view.

Moral judgments about historical figures. The other type of opinions of a historical nature consists of moral judgments about the conduct of historical figures. In this area, I should, first of all, distinguish implicit and explicit moral judgments. Implicit moral judgments are woven into the historian's vocabulary. Such judgments are either conscious (and therefore avoidable) or unconscious (and therefore partly unavoidable although training can reduce their impact). Explicit moral judgments are more complicated in the sense that there is no agreement about this category of opinions among historians: Are they desirable? Should the past be understood *or* understood *and* judged? This is a very old debate that has virtually split the historical profession. In offering a middle position, the human rights perspective provides a coherent solution to this debate. Let me clarify.

The noncoercion principle, which tells us that the right to express opinions includes the right *not* to express opinions, is applicable to moral judgments about past historical figures because they are a subcategory of opinions. It implies that passing moral judgment on the conduct of historical figures is a right, not a responsibility. This means that both those who defend the desirability of passing moral judgment and those who reject it are right, but it also means that they cannot compel others to adopt their views. The human rights perspective thus offers a good solution to this old debate.

---

[120] Ibid., §49. See also SRFEX, Report [Disinformation], §38; IMFE, Joint Declaration ["Fake news"], §2a; Article 19, *'Hate Speech'*, 28, 32–34. The right to err can be traced back to John Stuart Mill. See Mill, 9–32. For a philosophy of mistakes, see Dennett, 19–28.

If historians decide to exercise their right to pass judgment on the responsibility and guilt of perpetrators of past atrocities or draw moral lessons from them, they should do this responsibly, not recklessly. In a mitigated version, the Goldwater rule about public figures ("It is unethical for a psychiatrist to offer a professional opinion unless he or she has conducted an examination") is valid for historians as well. If, in contrast, they refuse to pass judgment, they could at least try, to the best of their ability, to indicate the *range* of well-founded moral judgments and, if applicable, which *type* of moral lessons to draw. The reason for this is that historians are experts who usually have studied these crimes deeper and longer than others. This responsibility is professional: It arises from their expert knowledge – and not from any human rights rule.[121]

Past public and private figures have to be judged differently. In line with what was said about public figures in Section 2, a quasi-universally accepted legal doctrine asserts that public figures – all those who play a role in public life, foremost political leaders – should tolerate more criticism than private citizens, not less. Accordingly, the UN Human Rights Committee "expresse[d] concern regarding laws on such matters as, lese majesty, *desacato*, disrespect for authority, disrespect for flags and symbols, defamation of the head of state and the protection of the honour of public officials . . . States Parties should not prohibit criticism of institutions, such as the army or the administration."[122] This concern extends to moral judgments that criticize *public* figures. In contrast, the relevance of disclosing personal data of *private* figures, deceased or not, is generally low and so is the passing of moral judgment on them. The low relevance of judging private figures, however, can be reversed when they become the subject of a biography (as has been increasingly the case since the advent of microhistory and subaltern history) or when the evaluation of what is illuminating, typical, or exceptional for an epoch or a milieu changes over time.

Opinions and hate speech. In Section 3, I discussed genocide denial (and more broadly, atrocity denial) in the context of breaches of the right to memory. A few words should now be added for historical writing. Historians and human rights scholars view genocide denial differently. For historians, genocide denial is a form of pseudohistory; for human rights scholars, it is a vehicle of defamation, discrimination, hostility, or violence.[123]

---

[121] See also Bloxham; Gorman. Bloxham distinguished six positions: neutralism (identical to what I call "understanding"), moral contextualism, moral relativism, moral internalism, presentism, and universalism (positions that are of part of what I call "judging").

[122] CCPR, General Comment 34, §§38, also §§34, 47.

[123] Accordingly, applications of Holocaust deniers to the ECtHR are systematically rejected. In doing so, the ECtHR does not resort to Art. 10 European Convention on Human Rights (freedom of expression), but to Art. 17 (the abuse clause), designed to counter the "enemies of democracy." The ECtHR has consistently viewed Holocaust denial as constituting advocacy

The threshold that transforms genocide denial into hate speech is crossed when it directly and publicly incites discrimination, hostility, and violence (including persecution, war, and genocide). This is a high threshold: Not all nonconformist historical research, not all negative stereotypes, not all offending speech with historical overtones constitutes hate speech. However, hate speech about past events may and will skillfully weave truthful elements into its stories in order to make it sound more convincing. It is fake investigation posing as genuine historical research or as legitimate political speech. This complicates the matter.

One of the criteria to separate genuine historical research from hate speech is *intent*.[124] If the intent of the authors is to incite discrimination, hostility, or violence toward some target group and if this is not carried out merely negligently or recklessly, but knowingly and willingly, their statements constitute hate speech. In contrast, if the genuine intent is evidence-based truth-seeking, it is not hate speech, even if that truth fails to convince others (in particular, other historians) or disturbs, shocks, or offends them. Another criterion is *imminence of risk* of discrimination, hostility, or violence against persons belonging to the targeted group and, consequently, the likelihood of harm inflicted on them. Of course, historians *exposing* past-related hate speech, for example of genocide deniers, and quoting from their works to prove this, are not deniers themselves as they do not endorse but rather rebut hate speech.[125]

4.4 Rights of Historians

So far, I have presented the human rights take on historical facts and opinions. In doing so, I have concentrated on history, not on historians. This is for good reason because historians are not the only ones who produce historical facts and opinions. The human rights framework is a general one, valid for all information and ideas regardless of whether they relate to the past, present, or future, and for all persons who process them, regardless of any professional expertise.

Let us now focus on the historians themselves. It is easy to see that they have two types of rights: human rights and professional rights. To begin with, they have human rights as everyone does. Some of these are of vital interest for the exercise of their profession. I have already extensively discussed the rights to freedom of thought, opinion, information, and expression. Let us therefore look briefly at other crucial human rights, such as the rights to peaceful assembly and

---

of National Socialism, a totalitarian doctrine incompatible with democracy and human rights and falling outside the scope of free expression protected under Art. 10.

[124] OCHRH, Rabat Plan, §22, proposed a six-part threshold test for defining hate speech: context, speaker, intent, content, reach of speech, and likelihood (including imminence) of harm.

[125] Mendel, "Negotiating," 53, 55, 56 (discussing ECtHR, Jersild).

association, and copyright. Let us also digress a while on their professional rights, and academic freedom in particular.

Peaceful assembly and association, and the historical debate. Stipulated in Articles 21 and 22 ICCPR, the rights to peaceful assembly and association are extensions of the right to free expression and basically governed by the same permissible restrictions clause. They articulate the right of all individuals to meet, discuss, protest, and organize themselves. Under these rights, history-related meetings, demonstrations, and associations can proceed as they see fit, as long as they develop peaceful activities and organize membership on a voluntary basis. Their primary function is to enable robust historical debate in all its forms.[126]

Let us dwell a little longer on this notion of *historical debate*. A "debate about history" is a confrontation of adversarial opinions about the past. If the debate is private, we call it a conversation or a dialogue. If it is public, it can be critical or not: it is only critical if the historical evidence is respected, the logic of arguments tested, and a diversity of evidence-based interpretations tolerated. Any typology of public debates about history should distinguish direct exchanges between two or more persons in oral or written form (teaching, publications, discussions at congresses, in the media, on the streets) from indirect exchanges between two or more persons separated in time. The latter range from one-directional criticism to bi- and multidirectional discussions in a meta-community with participants, some of whom are alive and some of whom are dead (but the debate then engages with the works left by the latter). Direct as well as indirect debates can take place between experts (the academic debate), nonexperts (the lay debate), or a mixture of both (for example, the historical debate in media outlets, courtrooms, government cenacles). They range from civilized exchanges to heated controversies. Some of the more polemical ones receive martial names such as "Historikerstreit" (battle of the historians), "memory wars" (a chain of public debates intended to determine how a given set of historical events is to be publicly remembered), or "history wars" (a chain of public debates intended to determine how a given set of historical events is to be studied and taught).

Special attention should be given to those who initiate and end debates of history. Quite a few times, debates are not started according to the procedural and moral rules of discourse proposed by such eminent social philosophers as Jürgen Habermas or Naomi Oreskes in their inspiring works about discourse and science.[127] Many debates are distorted by political power and manipulated

---

[126] SRFPAA, Joint Report, §§37–49; SRFPAA, Ten Principles.

[127] Finlayson, 76–105; Oreskes, 53, 128–129, 133, 259–260, 275.

by lobby groups. They become targets of selective access strategies and inappropriate interventions and are transformed into debates about the present, in which history is but a pretext for political or other gain. In dictatorial countries, coercion and repression prevent open debate about controversial topics: Under such intimidating circumstances, free debate can only take place in sheltered or closed forums. Initiating debates can be manipulated, and so can ending them. In dictatorships, closing or discouraging debates compels critical participants to continue them in clandestinity. In democracies, disputes can be advanced or even settled with new sources, better arguments, or an astute re-examination of the debate itself,[128] but many disputes on broad questions are open-ended because of the possibility to derive multiple opinions from the same sets of facts. In these cases, consensus (if that is the goal at all) is impossible to reach: Any settlement of "the truth" has to be regarded as temporary and preliminary.

Under their responsibility to protect, States must create a safe and enabling environment in law and practice for debates, including historical debates. When balanced against other interests, the free-expression interest they represent is so strong that there is little scope for restrictions. As was noted in Section 2, the interest in a robust public debate about the past increases when public figures and victims of atrocity crimes are involved.

Public debates about the past are not only strong practices of the freedoms of expression, assembly, and association. Their value is also essential for the quality of historical scholarship. The mere prospect of criticism makes historians vigilant about the merits of their own approach. The permanent possibility of review by colleagues in one's disciplinary community and by others keeps historians on their toes, and by enhancing the intersubjectivity of historical scholarship, it helps achieve a basic but essential degree of objectivity.[129]

Copyright. In some respects, copyright – one of the categories of intellectual property – is a human right. Indeed, Article 15.1(c) ICESCR provides the basis for a copyright regime: "The States Parties . . . recognize the right of everyone [t]o benefit from the protection of the moral and material interests resulting from any scientific, literary or artistic production of which he is the author." Copyright does not protect information and ideas as such but only their original expression in "any scientific, literary or artistic production." The right aims to encourage creative expression and scientific progress, emphasizing the personal character of many creations of the human mind and the durable link between creators and their creations.[130]

---

[128] Tucker, 1–4.   [129] Popper, 152–159.
[130] CESCR, General Comment 17, §§12–14, 39b, 44–45.

Crucially, Article 15.1(c) ICESCR distinguishes *moral and material interests*.[131] The material interests of copyright are best known: They consist of the economic benefits attached to the sale of a work. Economic claims are transferable to other persons and, in most cases, last until fifty to seventy years after the author's death. Once this period has expired, the work enters the public domain. The moral interests are different and, for my purposes, more important: They exist independently of the material interests, are nontransferable (except to heirs), do not expire, and include several rights. Two of these moral rights are human rights because they relate to the personality of the authors and their right to reputation (Article 17.1 ICCPR): the right of authors to be recognized as creators of their works unless they prefer anonymity or pseudonymity (called the right of authorship, paternity, or attribution) and their right to object to any distortion, mutilation, or other derogatory action in relation to their work, which would be prejudicial to their reputation (called the right of integrity or respect).[132] Other rights falling under the author's moral interests – such as rights of disclosure and withdrawal – are not human rights.

In the field of history, the author's moral interests have often been violated: The history of the censorship of history is replete with examples of data and manuscripts that were destroyed, stolen, pirated, or plagiarized; and of works that were published without the authors' name or consent, or under another author's name against their will.

In promoting authors' interests, copyright laws sometimes risk discouraging or stifling the "rights of others" interest, namely the latter's rights to access the information and ideas in the works of these authors (Article 19.2 ICCPR), and their rights to education (Article 13 ICESCR), to take part in cultural life (Article 15(a) ICESCR), and to enjoy the benefits of scientific progress and its applications (Article 15(b) ICESCR).[133] A helpful device to strike a balance between the copyright of authors and the rights of their audiences is the fair-use clause, under which small excerpts of the "scientific production" can be freely used for quotation, reviewing, and teaching purposes, on the condition that sources and authors are clearly referenced (for the preservation of moral interests). However, it remains controversial whether academic work that is publicly funded needs the incentivization of copyright at all.[134] Digital open-access publishing has broadened the scope of freely accessible and usable

---

[131] The idea of moral interests was first introduced in 1928 as Art. 6bis Berne Convention, which is also applicable to scientific works. Background in Burger.

[132] See World Intellectual Property Organization, 44–45, 296; SRCR, Report [Copyright policy], §§30–39; Burger, note 31.

[133] SRCR, Report [Copyright policy], §36; UNESCO 2009, §10.

[134] Centre for Law and Democracy, 35–36, 54.

historical knowledge, increasingly including unpublished data sets underlying these publications.

Unpublished materials pose their own problems, however. Manuscripts, correspondence, and confidential interviews are covered by the right to privacy (Article 17.1 ICCPR), but as this right is not absolute, these materials can sometimes be subpoenaed for use in the courtroom. The threat of forced disclosure of private scholarly communications through right to information requests or legal cases can chill or harm freedom of expression and academic freedom.[135]

From a copyright perspective, the genre of *commissioned history* poses a particular challenge. Commissioned history can be defined as a historical genre in which a commissioning individual or institution grants a temporary assignment, optionally including contracts and funding, to historians or others to do historical research and publish a collection of records or an analytical history. History commissioned *and* approved by official institutions is called *official history*. Contract clauses are important in this respect: They offer privileges (usually exclusive access to archives or witnesses), but if they lead to coercive interference in the research design, confidentiality of sources, mandatory pre-publication approval, and omission of authorship, they risk jeopardizing the historian's independence and impartiality.[136] Commissioned histories can also lead to reclassification of archival records. Thus, the genre carries high risks of pressure from the commissioning entity, whether the State or others.

Another problem relates to *Indigenous peoples*, who see copyright as a collective rather than individual right and whose customs often require them not to publicly disclose (sacred) objects and forms of knowledge. This may pose problems for historians and archaeologists who want to investigate their tangible and intangible heritage.[137] Whereas generally the interests of history and culture converge, here they diverge because the right of Indigenous peoples to take part in cultural life (Article 15.1(a) ICESCR) and their copyright (Article 15.1(c) ICESCR), when they entail confidentiality, have to be balanced against the right of scholars to access information and ideas (Article 19.2 ICCPR) and of others to enjoy the benefits of scientific progress (Article 15.1(b) ICESCR). This balance has shifted over time, with an increasing sensitivity to the views of Indigenous copyright holders.

Freedom of expression and academic freedom. The freedom of expression enjoyed by historians as human beings and the academic freedom enjoyed by

---

[135] The (limited) right of scholars to nondisclosure of their private communications is analogous to the (limited) right of journalists to nondisclosure of their sources.

[136] See also Berne Convention, Arts. 3(3), 14ter.1(1).

[137] SRCR, Report [Copyright policy], §§55–59.

them as academics are often confused.[138] Since the professionalization of history beginning in the nineteenth century, historians working at higher education institutions have enjoyed academic freedom: the freedom to teach and do research without internal or external interference.[139]

Academic freedom does not figure in either the ICCPR or ICESCR: It is not an explicit part of the family of human rights. This does not mean, however, that some of its dimensions are not deeply rooted in human rights. The strongest evidence for these roots is found in the ICESCR when it speaks about State responsibilities "to respect the freedom indispensable for scientific research and creative activity" (Article 15.3 ICESCR) and to "recognize the benefits to be derived from the encouragement and development of international contacts and co-operation in the scientific and cultural fields" (Article 15.4 ICESCR). However, the notion of "freedom indispensable for scientific research" is narrower than academic freedom because the latter also encompasses the freedom to teach; the notion is also larger because scientific research can be carried out outside academic institutions. Both State responsibilities are important preconditions for academic freedom, nevertheless. Other human rights, such as free expression (Article 19.2 ICCPR), peaceful assembly and association (Articles 21–22 ICCPR), and education (Article 13 ICESCR), are also prerequisites for, or components of, academic freedom but academic freedom as such is not mentioned in either the ICCPR or the ICESCR.

Although there is an increasing tendency within the UN to bestow autonomous human rights status upon academic freedom,[140] it is exactly what is says it is: a professional freedom of academics. It is governed by the same permissible restrictions clause as the right to freedom of expression, but with an additional restriction: It can only offer protection if it is used during a search for scientific truth. This professional freedom is strong: It belongs to individual scholars but because these scholars work at universities and similar higher education institutions, they also enjoy the additional protection of university autonomy. Let us now see where the regimes of freedom of expression and academic freedom differ with respect to a range of epistemological categories: truth, omission, confidentiality, secrecy, lie, ignorance, and mistake. This comparison will help dissipate the frequent confusion between both regimes.

Under *the freedom of expression regime* (Article 19 ICCPR), everyone is (obviously) allowed to tell the truth, but the protection of expression is not limited

---

[138] "Academic freedom" should not be confused with "intellectual freedom," which is a virtual synonym of the freedoms of thought and opinion (Arts. 18.1–19.1 ICCPR).

[139] UNESCO 1997, §27.

[140] CESCR, General Comment 25; SRFEX, Report [Freedom of expression aspects of academic freedom]; SRCR, Report [Right to participate in science]; SRRE, Report [Academic freedom].

to opinions that one considers truthful because on the one hand general prohibitions on the dissemination of false ideas are not allowed under the right to err principle, while on the other hand, it is legitimate not to express opinions that one believes to be true under the noncoercion principle. Furthermore, it is allowed and in some cases even obligatory to consider selected facts and opinions as "confidential" or "secret," for example, for reasons of privacy or national security. Lying – the intentional telling of untruths – sometimes violates the responsibility that comes with freedom of expression but, again, general bans on the dissemination of false ideas are not allowed. Lying is only blameworthy if it leads to a genuine risk of a specific harm such as defamation, fraud, or perjury. From a human rights perspective, laws should protect privacy and reputation (Article 17.2 ICCPR) and prohibit propaganda for war and hate speech (Article 20 ICCPR). In addition, under general law, fraud and perjury are prohibited.[141] Factual ignorance and factual errors are no problem: Everyone has the right not to know something or to be wrong.

To sum up, we should distinguish statements of opinion, true statements of fact, and untrue statements of fact. Almost all statements of opinion and almost all true statements of fact are protected, the main exception for my purposes being true historical facts that invade someone's privacy or threaten national security. Untrue factual statements are also protected, provided they do not lead to specific harms. This is, in a nutshell, the epistemological regime of freedom of expression.

The *epistemological regime of academic freedom* deviates from the freedom of regime – and always for the same reason: The honest pursuit of truth is the central mission of higher education.[142] Under the academic freedom regime, therefore, there is a responsibility to tell the truth to the best of one's ability, even if it will always be a provisional version of it. Academic freedom can only be appealed to on its behalf. As indicated in Section 4.3, we must supplement the professional responsibilities to seek and tell the (provisional) truth with another professional responsibility that academics worldwide have agreed upon, namely, to submit one's findings to peer review. Peer review is what makes science a social, not individual, process. Only through criticism and debate can we separate the true from the untrue and the plausible from the implausible, temporarily or permanently. Except for an important phase of private thought in the *forum internum*, the quality of research floats on the cork of permanent review and debate as tests for truth-seeking and truth-telling.[143]

Within this strict truth regime, academics are exceptionally permitted to omit certain facts, whether or not in the form of confidentiality and secrecy

---

[141] See Mendel, "Negotiating," 61.

[142] UNESCO 1997, §33: "Academic freedom carries with it the duty to use that freedom in a manner consistent with the scholarly obligation to base research on an honest search for truth."

[143] See, e.g., Williams, 217.

agreements. This is legitimate if they need to protect the privacy of their research subjects or if national security and public order interests are likely to be at risk. However, because truth-seeking is their core activity, openness is the rule and academics should use this privilege of silence as sparingly as possible and always after conscientiously balancing the interests involved.[144] Academics, moreover, can omit opinions (in the form of comments, interpretations, and judgments), for example, if omission serves focus and clarity of style, or if they feel that their opinions have not matured enough. This liberty, too, must be used cautiously, as research without interpretation is only mere accumulation of data.

Whereas silence and omission are sometimes permitted, an academic freedom regime prohibits lying at all times. This does not only apply to lying about facts; opinions must not be misleading either – they must stay true to the facts and be plausible, so as to advance reliable knowledge.

Finally, the academic attitude toward ignorance and error is complex. There is some tolerance for factual ignorance, but it is limited because the responsibility to stay informed about the state of the art in one's discipline is permanent. Likewise, there is tolerance for reasonable factual errors: No one is perfect and everyone makes mistakes. If mistakes become serial or large-scale, however, occasional negligence turns into gross negligence or even malice, and in this there cannot be mercy. The attitude toward ignorance and error in the field of opinions is entirely different. Science is an open-ended operation, a mission whose outcome is always uncertain. Ignorance is ingrained in scientific inquiry. Scientific truths and theories are provisional, constructed within bounds, and contested, not absolute. And the right to err – the right to systematically work on ideas that prove unfruitful in the end – is essential. Academics are protected by academic freedom when they state opinions that pass peer review but prove to be implausible and incredible in the end, but not when they keep defending the same opinions after peers have convincingly rejected them – unless new elements change the initial test situation.

What should I conclude from this epistemological analysis? Academic freedom incorporates all the restrictions of freedom of expression, but on top of that obligates academics to honest truth-seeking and truth-telling. Freedom of expression is a necessary but not sufficient condition for academic freedom. In other words, academic freedom is a special subcategory of free expression. Academic freedom and academic debate are far more regulated and controlled than free expression and public debate. Therefore, equating academic freedom with free expression is a fallacy.[145]

---

[144] De Baets 2009, 150–151.
[145] See also CESCR, General Comment 25; SRFEX, Report [Academic freedom]; Barendt; Beaud, 611–615; Williams, 217.

4.5 Responsibilities of Historians

Over the years, many principles have been proposed to organize the duties and responsibilities of historians. One such organizing principle emphasized their *scope* and subdivided them into professional, civic, social, cultural, political, and other responsibilities. A second principle highlighted the *addressees* and subdivided them into responsibilities toward past generations, present generations, and future generations. A third principle foregrounded their *performers* and subdivided them into responsibilities of individual historians and responsibilities of the community of historians. A fourth principle, finally, emphasized the *context* and distinguished responsibilities in times of war, during public emergencies, and in peacetime.

None of these organizing principles will be used in the new theory of historians' responsibilities presented here, although they are compatible with it and many of their key elements return in it. The theory is based on human rights and distinguishes three main responsibilities, using their *performative nature* as its organizing principle: One responsibility requires them "to respect," another "to protect," and a third "to promote." The theory is a general human-rights based theory of responsibilities, applicable to all States and individuals,[146] which I already used when discussing memory-related responsibilities in Section 3 and which I will now apply to history-related responsibilities and particularly to historians' responsibilities.

The relationship between human rights and responsibilities. The most important human rights instruments – the UDHR, ICCPR, and ICESCR – refer to duties and responsibilities. They do so profusely to duties and responsibilities of States and sparsely to those of individuals. From the outset, human rights were intended to shield against the arbitrary power of States, and therefore the drafters of these human rights instruments were rather explicit about States' responsibilities but not about individual responsibilities because they feared that States would use any clauses about the duties and responsibilities of individuals to restrict rather than promote the latter's human rights.[147]

The UDHR contains only two responsibilities: the responsibility of all to act in a spirit of brotherhood (Article 1) and the responsibility of individuals to the community (Article 29). The ICCPR and the ICESCR have a largely identical preamble which refers to both State and individual responsibilities: In one paragraph it says that it is "the obligation of States under the Charter of the United Nations to promote universal respect for, and observance of, human

---

[146] See OHCHR, International Human Rights Law. To my knowledge, the triad first appeared in 1997 (namely in Maastricht Guidelines, §6).

[147] See SRFEX, Report [Challenges], §8; Cassell, 59–63.

rights and freedoms" and, in a following paragraph, echoing the UDHR, it stipulates that "the individual, having duties to other individuals and to the community to which he belongs, is under a responsibility to strive for the promotion and observance of the rights recognized in the present Covenant."

Since the Covenants ask all individuals to assume the responsibility to promote human rights, society can rightfully make claims upon its historians to help promote some of these rights. In particular, the (human) rights of everyone to access information, receive education, participate in the cultural life of the community, and share in the benefits of scientific progress – discussed in Section 4.4 – seem to provide a basis for society to make some responsibility claims upon its historians.[148]

Interestingly, Article 19.3 ICCPR, which contains the permissible restrictions clause, clarifies the *basis of our responsibilities theory*. It stipulates that "The exercise of the rights [to freedom of expression] carries with it special duties and responsibilities. It may therefore be subject to certain restrictions ... " This clause throws light on the source of the responsibilities held by individuals: Individuals have responsibilities *because* they have rights. Rights are prior to, and the rationale for, responsibilities. The logic of the relationship lies in the fact that the right has to be guaranteed to the maximum and that any restrictions flowing from individual responsibilities when exercising it must be carefully justified.[149] In short, a human rights perspective on the historian's ethics expressly links the responsibilities of historians to human rights – something strangely absent in most theories of ethics for historians that exclusively focus on virtues and responsibilities.

Responsibilities, duties, and virtues. Strictly speaking, "duties" are general ethical or moral obligations and "responsibilities" obligations that are legally binding under existing international law,[150] but both terms are used interchangeably here – as is general practice.[151] Therefore, when I speak of responsibilities, I also mean duties and obligations. With legal philosopher Ronald Dworkin I can distinguish two major types of responsibilities: responsibilities to oneself (or virtues) and responsibilities toward others (or relational responsibilities).[152] As for virtues,[153] I might further distinguish *recommended and essential virtues*. Curiosity, modesty, and open-mindedness would be recommended intellectual virtues. If historians do not comply with them, the quality of their work may suffer, but no great

---

[148] Arts. 19, 26–27 UDHR, corresponding to Art. 19.2 ICCPR and Arts. 13.1, 15.1(a)–(b) ICESCR.
[149] Cassell, 59–60.   [150] Foqué, 25–27.   [151] See, e.g., SRHRHR, Art. 1.
[152] In his theory of responsibility, Dworkin, 102–104, distinguishes virtue responsibilities (subdivided into intellectual, practical, ethical, and moral responsibilities) and relational responsibilities (subdivided into causal, assignment, liability, and judgmental responsibilities).
[153] For the virtues of historians, see Paul, 1–8, 52–53.

harm is done to others. In contrast, honesty (an ethical virtue) and accuracy (an epistemic virtue) are essential virtues because noncompliance with them (for example, when historians lie or act with reckless disregard for facts) may lead to harmful consequences for others – and for history as a discipline.

Judges ruling on complaints against what historians have said or written will evaluate a defense of the latter based on virtues as a sign of good faith but a defense based on relational responsibilities will be more convincing.[154] They will almost always refrain from determining "the historical truth" themselves. Instead, they usually verify "procedural aspects" of the historical work that is the target of a complaint: whether historians carried out their research about their subjects of study honestly in accordance with the public interest and with generally accepted standards of accuracy that prudent historians usually observe.[155]

We see that essential virtues such as honesty and accuracy occupy a middle ground between recommended virtues and relational responsibilities because failing to comply with them may harm others. The ethical framework, then, is clear: When historians act, they are protected by rights, guided by virtues, and restricted by responsibilities. Rights set claims, virtues set best practices, responsibilities set floors. Together they foster *responsible history*. We may now ask: What exactly *are* these responsibilities?

The responsibilities of States toward history and historians. The responsibilities of States toward history should be read in conjunction with their responsibilities toward memory (Section 3). A State *responsibility to respect* history and historians means that States should abstain from direct or complicit involvement in attacks on historians, including history educators, memory activists, archaeologists, archivists, and heritage professionals.[156] The State has also responsibilities to respect the freedom of scientific research and to recognize the benefits of international scientific cooperation, discussed in Section 4.4.[157] A State *responsibility to protect* requires States to proactively take measures to prevent, condemn, prohibit, investigate, and prosecute attacks on historians and related professionals at risk from third parties, and to offer remedies for the victims of such attacks.[158] A State *responsibility to promote* requires States to set up a solid and equitable legislative framework for educational and research institutions that execute history-related work, and for archives and museums and similar cultural institutions. It also requires States to take policy measures to foster development of the field.

---

[154] See also Mendel, "Reflections," 60–61.   [155] De Baets 2009, 85–89.

[156] Attacks on historians are threats or uses of force by State or non-State actors against historians or their work with the intent to silence them.

[157] ICESCR, Arts. 15.3–15.4.   [158] CCPR, General Comment 31, §8.

The responsibilities of historians toward history and historians. If I pass from States to the level at which historians operate, I discern an analogy. If historians as a community want to operate autonomously, they have to accept responsibilities analogous to those assigned to States:

- *A responsibility to respect history and historians.* The responsibility to respect *history* requires respect for the principle of scientific integrity when approaching the past as historians.[159] Integrity – the attitude of being honest and accurate and not acting corruptly – implies that being a historian is coterminous with working in good faith; historians acting in bad faith are not historians. This integrity principle is so obvious that it is seldom made explicit. In the Faurisson case (a case of Holocaust denial), the UN Human Rights Committee stressed the principle of honesty in historical research,[160] thus essentially echoing the views of Max Weber, who spoke about "intellektuelle Rechtschaffenheit" (intellectual integrity) as the central scholarly value as early as 1918.[161] In UNESCO's words, the task of responsible science is "an honest search for truth."[162] A responsibility to respect *historians* means that one should always respect the rights of other historians and of students, and ensure a fair discussion of contrary views.[163]
- *A responsibility to protect history and historians.* This responsibility requires historians to *oppose* abuses of history and attacks on history by third parties.[164] Among the most serious abuses are the intentional denial or misrepresentation (fabrication, falsification, plagiarism) of historical facts and opinions; among the most serious attacks are "crimes against history," attacks that are criminal according to domestic or international law, for example when historians are assassinated for political reasons. Abuses of history and attacks on historians do not only harm historians but also history itself. Their chilling effects usually result in fewer and less active speakers and fewer and less receptive listeners in the historical debate than otherwise would have been the case.

The responsibility to *oppose* attacks on, and abuses of, history can be broken down into a series of steps ranging from preventing to investigating, disclosing, and sanctioning these abuses and attacks as well as expressing solidarity with those attacked.[165] The first of these steps – prevention – is

---

[159] For integrity, see Alfaix Assis; Bevir, 142–150; Gibbons; Jay; Raphael and Zachariah; Williams, 84–148.

[160] CCPR, Faurisson, concurring opinion of Evatt, Kretzmer, and Klein, §§6, 10. See also De Baets 2017, 45–46.

[161] Weber.   [162] UNESCO 1997, §33.   [163] Ibid., §33.

[164] Attacks on history are defined in note 156. Abuses of history are uses of history with the intent to *deceive* for political or other purposes: see De Baets 2009, 9–48. See also International Committee of Historical Sciences, Art. 1.

[165] De Baets 2009, 35–39; De Baets 2023a, 324.

a responsibility for all historians, but the other steps are usually carried out collectively by historical associations, institutions, or journals, or by the judicial apparatus. Prevention of abuse is fostered through the cultivation of a careful and honest work habit in the first place, especially by generously acknowledging intellectual debts in notes and references, and by carefully distinguishing quotation and paraphrase. Standard-setting through the development of professional codes of ethics is also important. Awareness can be raised by teaching professional ethics to students, including research into and teaching about the history of the attacks on and abuses of history. Solidarity with colleagues at risk requires first and foremost defending the latter's human and professional rights.

• *A responsibility to promote history.* This responsibility requires the creation of favorable conditions for research and teaching, in the first place by establishing equitable research ecosystems and high-quality education curricula free from indoctrination. It also requires the arrangement, to the extent possible, of responsible and dignified scientific and public debates about the dark sides of history, including its atrocities. Occasionally, human rights bodies have suggested how the responsibility to promote has to be understood. The UN Human Rights Committee has emphasized the principles of objectivity, neutrality, and nondiscrimination in (history) education.[166] And the UN Special Rapporteur on cultural rights noted that history teaching should be free from political or religious indoctrination.[167] Indoctrination is seen as a violation of the right to education (Article 13 ICESCR).

Discussion of the responsibilities of historians. Whereas the responsibilities to respect and promote defend responsible history, the responsibility to protect fights irresponsible history. The responsibility to respect is the most important of all: It is a responsibility of result without which the responsibilities to protect and promote become meaningless. For how can one protect and promote history if one does not respect it in the first place? In contrast, the responsibilities to protect and promote are responsibilities of effort, of means, and of conduct governed by risk-reducing precautionary and due diligence principles. Within the ambit of the responsibility to protect, the responsibility to prevent is weightier than the responsibilities to investigate, disclose, sanction, or express solidarity because all historians are able to contribute to prevention.

The responsibility to respect is absolute: It cannot be waived under any circumstances. In contrast, historians' responsibilities to protect and promote can be tempered by three factors. To begin with, they are mitigated by the degree to which historians' rights are respected. We have responsibilities

---

[166] In CCPR, Hartikainen, §10.4; CCPR, Ross, §11.6. See also De Baets 2017, 44–45.
[167] SRCR, Report [Writing and teaching of history], §§64–70, 86–88.

because we have rights, and therefore it is logical to assume that responsibilities to protect and promote diminish when rights diminish. If historians' rights are not, or not completely, respected, and in particular if their physical safety is threatened and if they live under duress, their responsibilities to protect and promote diminish to the same degree.

Second, the responsibilities to protect and promote are tempered by the degree of autonomy they are granted by society when it requires them to promote specific human rights. In order to do so, historians need a margin of liberty. There can be no accountability toward society and no protection or promotion of human rights without some substantial form of autonomy (including academic freedom).

Finally, historians' responsibilities to protect and promote are toned down by their potentially conflicting character: Historians fulfill several social and professional roles and belong to diverse local, national, and global communities – and, therefore, responsibilities emanating from these roles and communities may conflict and should be balanced against each other. Virtues, for example, can compete: "Complete honesty may clash with prudence, justice with compassion, benevolence with fortitude."[168]

This conflict of responsibilities can be clearly illustrated in the field of history education. According to Article 13.1 ICESCR, the right to education should be realized in the service of human rights, international understanding, and peace. According to the historians' own set of responsibilities, however, historians should respect the integrity of history, that is, they should honestly search for the historical truth. These aims – human rights and peace versus integrity and truth – can conflict because the findings of historical research (including those taught in the classroom) often do not point to respect for human rights, international understanding, or peace but rather to conflict and violence. While the aims of the ICESCR are certainly valid, reading them dogmatically into history can distort the latter. And this may eventually discourage history teachers and students from embracing them.

This is, in a nutshell, how a human-rights based theory of historians' responsibilities looks like. It uses the logic of human rights theory to formulate the fundamental responsibilities of historians. And these form the basis upon which other responsibilities can be built.

4.6 Conclusion

International human rights law offers clear epistemological and ethical guidelines for historians. At the epistemological level, human rights are strict for facts and protective of opinions. For my purposes, "opinions" include memories,

---

[168] Gibbons, 11.

interpretations of past events, and moral judgments about historical figures. In the human rights approach toward these historical opinion types the noncoercion and right to err principles are pivotal. According to the noncoercion principle, one is not obligated to express opinions about the past, meaning that from a human rights perspective chronicles or annals – fact-centered historical genres with relatively low levels of interpretation – are as valuable as more sophisticated historical analyses and commentaries. But once they are uttered, the right to err principle comes into play. Opinions merit strong protection even when they prove implausible in the end. However, if uttered as part of an academic discourse, opinions are always subject to peer review tests and should be dropped if peers conclusively reject them.

Human rights ethics presents a broader framework than historians usually do because from the outset – and in contrast to the latter's narrower theories – it focuses not only on responsibilities but also, and primarily, on rights by postulating that human rights are prior to responsibilities. However, most human rights are not absolute and therefore they are subject to a narrow range of permissible restrictions, which in turn requires a fine-tuned regime of responsibilities. In its structure, though not in its content, this regime is identical for States as for the community of historians: It consists of coherent responsibilities to respect, protect, and promote.

General Conclusion

A human rights view of the past provides original insights that can be used to study history under a new light. Section 2 revealed that some human rights principles restrain the temporal scope under which to observe the past and others enlarge it, giving rise to a mixed time regime. This reflects the age-old struggle of human beings to cope with the effects of the passage of time on the availability of records and with the complex moral, legal, and historical evaluation of atrocity crimes.

Section 3 demonstrated that the human rights view offers consistent answers for an impressive range of questions that arise when we act in the area of memory. These questions are: Do dead persons have human rights? What is the relationship between free thought, opinion, and memory? Is memory a right? Can it be restricted and when and how? Is memory a right that comes with responsibilities or a responsibility rather than a right? What does this responsibility look like for individuals and for the State? How to balance it with other interests? What is a responsible memory? Are memory laws appropriate and when? What is the role of noncoercion in memory issues? Is there a right to be remembered? Is there a right to silence? Is there a right to forget? Is there a right to be forgotten? Are memory and tradition allies or rivals of history? Does the denial of atrocity crimes breach the right to memory? Seen from a human rights perspective, these questions are interrelated and answered from a logic that is acceptable not only to historians but also to their *Umwelt*, including the judicial authorities who decide about such issues when historians land in the dock.

Section 4 tried to illuminate various problems in the domain of history. It made a plea to rehabilitate historical facts, especially existential facts about life and death, given their vital importance to millions of people who have become victims of human rights violations around the world and who want to find out the truth of what happened. It recognized the fundamental role of the right to err in historical interpretation. It showed how to approach moral judgment in history, including absence of such judgment. It clarified the difference between historical research and hate speech posing as historical research. In addition, it dwelled on the ethics of historians, that is, their rights and responsibilities. It identified those human rights that are of special interest to them. It dispelled frequent misunderstandings about academic freedom and its difference with freedom of expression. It argued that the rights of historians trigger their responsibilities and proposed a new theory of the basic responsibilities of historians. All of these insights help design solutions to the problems of time, memory, and history that historians and others confront.

But it does not stop there. The ultimate purpose of a human rights view of the past lies elsewhere. It is to find a solid basis for the ethical imperative of "never again," shorthand for the *nonrecurrence principle*. The entire human rights campaign is driven by this all-pervading future-oriented principle that frequently figures in international treaties. It means that everyone has a responsibility to prevent past human rights violations from recurring in the future. In order not to lose sight of this final purpose, the UN appointed, in 2011, a Special Rapporteur on truth, justice and reparation, who authored reports on guarantees of nonrecurrence with suggestions ranging from simple precautions to sophisticated early-warning systems.[169] The nonrecurrence principle attempts to integrate insights derived from historical comparisons and analogies into the creation of nonrecurrence guarantees and therefore into the empowerment of present and future generations to live peaceful and good lives. If the nonrecurrence principle as the final purpose of "the human rights school of history" is compared to the purposes of many other schools of history, it is modest but realistic because it is not oriented toward promising golden futures but toward avoiding cycles of

---

[169] See SRTJR, Report [Guarantees]; SRTJR, Report [Prevention] 2017 and 2018. See also ARSIWA, Art. 30(b), on nonrepetition. For overviews of nonrecurrence guarantees, see Impunity Principles, Principles 35, 36e, 38; Reparation Principles, Principle 23. See also OHCHR, "History and Human Rights as our Guide."

disaster and catastrophe. For this reason, human rights can be called a value system and a world view, but not a utopia.

However, the nonrecurrence principle has led to much confusion and unnecessary delusions: It does not denote – and never did – a responsibility of result, but one of effort. The pledge of "never again" refers to the determination with which to pursue the ultimate purpose (through fulfilling responsibilities to remember, prevent, investigate, and prosecute), not to the certainty that atrocities will disappear forever. Indeed, given the infinite variety of barbarity and cruelty and the rapid evolution of technological means to afflict them, past patterns of human rights violations are often poor predictors of future ones, even if some contemporary wars seem to repeat familiar cycles of violence. Alongside the twin dangers of anachronism and hindsight bias, briefly discussed in Section 2.2, two almost opposite obstacles to nonrecurrence are the Lucas critique and the prevention paradox. The *Lucas critique*, a critique of macroeconomic policy named after Nobel prize laureate Robert Lucas who was trained as a historian, can be applied to the notion of historical lessons. If we were rational, the argument goes, we would seek to reduce the impact of negative historical events (such as war). And if we did that long enough, they would disappear: The lessons would have a self-canceling effect, meaning that historical information would become useless for predicting the future. However, because many of these negative historical events continue to occur, we must conclude that we are not so rational and do not learn (much) from them. The *prevention paradox* is also an obstacle, but opposite to the Lucas critique: It assumes that it is possible to draw lessons from the past. But paradoxically, if such lessons produce preventive effects, the crimes and suffering thus prevented become untraceable. If the lessons of history are heeded, they prevent suffering, but if suffering decreases, how can one then prove that it was the result of such lessons learned in the first place? If the mission is to avoid and prevent the mistakes of the past, positive results are often untraceable, with the risk of skewing the balance negatively. But absence of evidence is not evidence of absence.

Despite these serious obstacles, historical awareness – the extraordinary capability to locate events in a long-term perspective – is a powerful tool. As integral forms of the right to freedom of expression, the rights to memory and history stimulate a responsible historical awareness. They are necessary conditions for prevention and nonrecurrence: "lest we forget" precedes "never again." Historians in particular can contribute professionally to repairing recent and remote historical injustice. This is so because, if done responsibly, a human rights-inspired historiography has several potential effects:

- *A substantive effect.* It helps replace, through critical historical research and education, distorted accounts of the past that fuel hatred and incite violence.

- *An epistemic effect*. It helps offer new historical information and new evidence-based interpretations of the past and, in doing so, helps discontinue silence, secrecy, denial, and lies surrounding past wrongdoing.
- *A reparative effect*. It helps provide symbolic reparation for victims of historical injustice and for society at large by replacing distorted historical facts and opinions with responsible ones.
- *An awareness effect*. It helps make present and future generations aware of historical injustice and offer them glimpses of historical justice.
- *An educational effect*. It helps explain the injustice of past generations to present and future generations.
- *A political effect*. It helps opt for a democratic political regime. Indeed, historians and related professionals have a political duty to support democratic societies because these societies offer better guarantees for human rights, including freedom of expression about the past, and, consequently, for the sustained exercise and enduring progress of historical writing, than nondemocratic societies. Conversely, the right to free expression about the past is a necessary condition for a pluralistic democratic awareness – itself a condition for the creation of a culture favorable to a robust democratic society – on the condition that this right is exercised responsibly when memorialization is practiced and historical accounts of democracy and of historical injustice are produced. In addition, historical findings can fuel important political debates and contribute to government transparency and accountability for State behavior in the past and therefore to trust in democratic political institutions. The hypothesis here is that responsibly exercised memory and history become imbued with a democratic spirit that in turn nurtures a democratic culture.[170]

International human rights law contains a set of principles and a logic that can be applied to the past. If it *is* carefully applied – in full awareness of the distortion risks it entails – it creates a coherent perspective to solve old problems in new ways and to candidly face the past and future.

---

[170] De Baets 2015. See also UNESCO 1997, § 27.

Bibliography

1. United Nations [UN] Instruments

International Bill of Human Rights

International Covenant on Civil and Political Rights, UN General Assembly Resolution 2200(XXI)A (1966) [ICCPR].

International Covenant on Economic, Social and Political Rights, UN General Assembly Resolution 2200(XXI)A (1966) [ICESCR].

Universal Declaration of Human Rights, UN General Assembly Resolution 217 (III)A (1948) [UDHR].

Treaties

Convention on the Non-Applicability of Statutory Limitations to War Crimes and Crimes against Humanity, UN General Assembly Resolution 2391 (XXIII) (1968).

Convention on the Prevention and Punishment of the Crime of Genocide, UN General Assembly Resolution 260(III) (1948) [Genocide Convention].

International Convention for the Protection of All Persons from Enforced Disappearance, UN General Assembly Resolution 61/177 (2006) [Disappearance Convention].

International Convention on the Elimination of All Forms of Racial Discrimination, UN General Assembly Resolution 2106(XX)A (1965) [ICERD].

Vienna Convention on the Law of Treaties (1969) [VCLT].

Vienna Convention on Succession of States in Respect of Treaties (1978).

Committee on Economic, Social and Cultural Rights [CESCR]

General Comment 17 [Authorship] (E/C.12/GC/17) (2005).

General Comment 21 [Taking part in cultural life] (E/C.12/GC/21) (2009).

General Comment 25 [Science and economic, social and cultural rights] (E/C.12/GC/25) (2020).

Human Rights Committee [CCPR]

General Comment 11 [Prohibition of propaganda for war and inciting national, racial or religious hatred] (A/38/40) (1983).

General Comment 16 [Rights to privacy and reputation] (HRI/GEN/1/Rev.1) (1988).

General Comment 20 [Torture] (HRI/GEN/1/Rev.1) (1992).

General Comment 22 [Freedoms of thought, conscience and religion] (CCPR/C/21/Rev.1/Add.4) (1993).

General Comment 26 [Continuity of obligations] (CCPR/C/21/Rev.1/Add.8/Rev.1) (1997).

General Comment 28 [Equality of rights between men and women] (CCPR/C/21/Rev.1/Add.10) (2000).

General Comment 29 [Derogations during a state of emergency] (CCPR/C/21/Rev.1/Add.11) (2001).

General Comment 31 [General legal obligation] (CCPR/C/21/Rev.1/Add. 13) (2004).

General Comment 34 [Freedoms of opinion and expression] (CCPR/C/GC/34) (2011).

General Comment 36 [Right to life] (CCPR/C/GC/36) (2019).

Communications

Cifuentes v. *Chile* (1536/2006) (2009).

F.A.J. and B.M.R.A v. *Spain* (3599/2019) (2020).

Faurisson v. *France* (550/1993) (1996).

Hartikainen v. *Finland* (40/1978) (1981).

K.K. and others v. *Russia* (2912/2016) (2019).

Quinteros v. *Uruguay* (107/1981) (1990).

Ross v. *Canada* (736/1997) (2000).

Schedko v. *Belarus* (886/1999) (2003).

Human Rights Council [HRC]

Preliminary Study on Promoting Human Rights and Fundamental Freedoms through a Better Understanding of Traditional Values of Humankind (A/HRC/AC/8/4 [2011]; A/HRC/AC/9/2 [2012]).

Promoting Human Rights and Fundamental Freedoms through a Better Understanding of Traditional Values of Humankind: Resolutions (A/HRC/RES/12/21 [2009]; A/HRC/RES/16/3 [2011]; A/HRC/21/3 [2012]).

Study of the Human Rights Council Advisory Committee on Promoting Human Rights and Fundamental Freedoms through a Better Understanding of Traditional Values of Humankind (A/HRC/22/71) (2012).

Summary of Information from States Members of the United Nations and Other Relevant Stakeholders on Best Practices in the Application of Traditional Values while Promoting and Protecting Human Rights and Upholding Human Dignity (A/HRC/24/22) (2013).

International Court of Justice [ICJ]

Legal Consequences for States of the Continued Presence of South Africa in Namibia (South West Africa) Notwithstanding Security Council Resolution 276 (1970), Advisory Opinion, *ICJ Reports 1971*.

Legal Consequences of the Construction of a Wall in the Occupied Palestinian Territory, Advisory Opinion, *ICJ Reports 2004*.

Legality of the Threat or Use of Nuclear Weapons, Advisory Opinion, *ICJ Reports 1996*.

Statute (1945).

International Law Commission [ILC]

Draft Articles on Responsibility of States for Internationally Wrongful Acts, with Commentaries (A/56/10) (2001) [ARSIWA].

Fragmentation of International Law: Difficulties Arising from the Diversification and Expansion of International Law (A/CN.4/L.682) (2006).

Peremptory Norms of General International Law (Jus Cogens) (A/74/10) (2019).

Principles of International Law Recognized in the Charter of the Nürnberg Tribunal and in the Judgment of the Tribunal, with Commentaries, in *Yearbook of the International Law Commission* (1950), 374–378.

Office on Genocide Prevention and the Responsibility to Protect [OGPRP]

Framework of Analysis for Atrocity Crimes: A Tool for Prevention (2014).

Office of the High Commissioner for Human Rights [OHCHR]

"History and Human Rights as our Guide," speech by United Nations High Commissioner for Human Rights Volker Türk (25 June 2024), www.ohchr.org/en/statements-andspeeches/2024/06/history-and-human-rights-our-guide.

International Human Rights Law (introductory website text), www.ohchr.org/en/instruments-and-mechanisms/international-human-rights-law.

Rabat Plan of Action on the Prohibition of Advocacy of National, Racial or Religious Hatred that Constitutes Incitement to Discrimination, Hostility or Violence (2012).

Right to the Truth: Report (A/HRC/5/7) (2007).

Right to the Truth: Study (E/CN.4/2006/91) (2006).

Rule-of-Law Tools for Post-Conflict States: Amnesties (2009).

Principles

Affirmation of the Principles of International Law Recognized by the Charter of the Nürnberg Tribunal, UN General Assembly Resolution 95(I) (1946) [Nuremberg Principles].

Basic Principles and Guidelines on the Right to a Remedy and Reparation for Victims of Gross Violations of International Human Rights Law and Serious Violations of International Humanitarian Law, UN General Assembly Resolution 60/147 (2005) [Reparation Principles].

Declaration of Basic Principles of Justice for Victims of Crime and Abuse of Power, UN General Assembly Resolution 40/34 (1985) [Victims Principles].

Declaration on the Protection of all Persons from Enforced Disappearance, UN General Assembly Resolution 47/133 (1992) [Disappearance Declaration].

Identification of Customary International Law (Annex), UN General Assembly Resolution 73/203 (2019).

Siracusa Principles on the Limitation and Derogation Provisions in the International Covenant on Civil and Political Rights (E/CN.4/1985/4) (1984) [Siracusa Principles].

Updated Set of Principles for the Protection and Promotion of Human Rights through Action to Combat Impunity (E/CN.4/2005/102/Add.1) (2005) [Impunity Principles].

Special Rapporteurs

Special Adviser on Prevention of Genocide [SAPG]
Combating Holocaust and Genocide Denial: Protecting Survivors, Preserving Memory, and Promoting Prevention – Policy Paper (2022).

Special Rapporteur on Cultural Rights [SRCR]
History and Memorialisation: Narratives about the Past Examined through the Lens of Cultural Rights (introductory website text), www.ohchr.org/en/special-procedures/sr-cultural-rights/history-and-memorialisation-narratives-about-past-examined-through-lens-cultural-rights.
Report [Copyright policy and right to science and culture] (A/HRC/28/57) (2014).
Report [Memorialization processes] (A/HRC/25/49) (2014).
Report [Right to participate in science] (A/HRC/55/44) (2024).
Report [Writing and teaching of history] (A/68/296) (2013).

Special Rapporteur on Freedom of Opinion and Expression [SRFEX]
Report [Challenges to freedom of expression] (A/71/373) (2016).
Report [Disinformation and freedom of expression] (A/HRC/47/25) (2021).
Report [Freedom of expression aspects of academic freedom] (A/75/261) (2020).
Report [Hate speech] (A/67/357) (2012).

Special Rapporteur on Freedom of Peaceful Assembly and of Association [SRFPAA]
Joint Report [Proper management of assemblies] (A/HRC/31/66) (2016).

Ten Principles for the Proper Management of Assemblies: Implementation Checklist (2016).

Special Rapporteur on Freedom of Religion or Belief [SRFRB]
Interim report [Freedom of thought] (A/76/380) (2021).
Report [Relationship between freedoms of belief and expression] (A/HRC/31/18) (2015).

Special Rapporteur on Human Rights and Human Responsibilities [SRHRHR]
Final Report [Human responsibilities] (E/CN.4/2003/105) (2003).

Special Rapporteur on the Right to Education [SRRE]
Report [Academic freedom] (A/HRC/56/58) (2024).

Special Rapporteur on Truth, Justice and Reparation [SRTJR]
Report [Guarantees of non-recurrence] (A/HRC/30/42) (2015).
Report [Prevention] (A/72/523) (2017).
Report [Prevention] (A/HRC/37/65) (2018).

UNESCO
History under Attack: Holocaust Denial and Distortion on Social Media (2022).
Recommendation Concerning the Status of Higher-Education Teaching Personnel (1997).
Venice Statement on the Right to Enjoy the Benefits of Scientific Progress and Its Applications (2009).

World Intellectual Property Organization
Berne Convention for the Protection of Literary and Artistic Works (originally 1886) (1979).
Guide to the Copyright and Related Rights Treaties Administered by WIPO and Glossary of Copyright and Related Rights Terms (2003).

2. Other Global Instruments

International Court of Arbitration [ICA]
Island of Palmas Case (Netherlands, USA), 1928, *Reports of International Arbitral Awards*, volume 2 (2006), 829–871.

International Criminal Court [ICC]
Rome Statute (1998; update 2021).
Trial Chamber II, Situation in the Democratic Republic of the Congo in the Case of the Prosecutor v. Germain Katanga (ICC–01/04–01/07):
– Order for Reparations (2017).

– Public Redacted Version of Decision on the Matter of the Transgenerational Harm Alleged by Some Applicants for Reparations Remanded by the Appeals Chamber in Its Judgment of 8 March 2018 (2018).

International Military Tribunal at Nuremberg [IMT]
Trial of the Major War Criminals before the International Military Tribunal, Nuremberg, 14 November 1945 – 1 October 1946, volume 1 (Nuremberg: Secretariat of the Tribunal, 1947).

International Humanitarian Law
Convention (II) with Respect to the Laws and Customs of War on Land (1899).
Geneva Conventions (1949) and their Additional Protocols (1977).
"List of Customary Rules of International Humanitarian Law," *International Review of the Red Cross*, 87 no. 857 (2005), 198–212.

International Mechanisms for Promoting Freedom of Expression [IMFE]
Joint Declaration [Access to information and secrecy legislation] (2004).
Joint Declaration [Freedom of expression and "fake news," disinformation and propaganda] (2017).
Joint Declaration [Universality and freedom of expression] (2014).

3. Regional Instruments

European Court of Human Rights [ECtHR]
Cultural Rights in the Case-Law of the European Court of Human Rights (2017).
Factsheet: Hate Speech (2023).
Guide on Article 17 of the European Convention of Human Rights [Prohibition of abuse of rights] (2024).

Cases
Jersild v. *Denmark* (15890/89) Grand Chamber (1994).
Lehideux and Isorni v. *France* (55/1997/839/1045) Grand Chamber (1998).
Perinçek v. *Switzerland* (27510/08) Grand Chamber (2015).
Suprun and others v. *Russia* (58029/12) (2024).

European Union
Court of Justice of the European Union, Judgment of the Court (Grand Chamber), 13 May 2014 – *Google* v. *AEPD and Costeja González* (2014) [CJEU].
Regulation (EU) 2016/679 of the European Parliament and of the Council of 27 April 2016 on the Protection of Natural Persons with Regard to the

Processing of Personal Data and on the Free Movement of Such Data, and Repealing Directive 95/46/EC (2016) [GDPR].

Inter-American Commission on Human Rights [IACHR]
Carmen Aguiar de Lapacó v. *Argentina*: Report no. 70/99 – Case 12.059 (1999).
Carmen Aguiar de Lapacó v. *Argentina*: Report no. 21/00 – Case 12.059 (2000).

Inter-American Court on Human Rights [IACtHR]
Velásquez Rodríguez Case: Judgment of July 29, 1988 (1988).

4. Literature

Alfaix Assis, Arthur, "Objectivity and the First Law of History Writing," *Journal of the Philosophy of History*, 13 (2019), 107–128.

Article 19, *Defining Defamation: Principles on Freedom of Expression and Protection of Reputation*. London: Article 19, 2017.

'Hate Speech' Explained: A Toolkit. London: Article 19, 2015.

Aswad, Evelyn Mary, "Loosing the Freedom to Be Human," *Columbia Human Rights Law Review*, 52 no. 1 (2020), 331–353.

Bán, Marina, and Uladzislau Belavusau, "Memory Laws," *Bloomsbury History: Theory and Method*. London: Bloomsbury Publishing, 2022, 1–27.

Baranowska, Grażyna, "How Long Does the Past Endure? 'Continuing Violations' and the 'Very Distant Past' Before the UN Human Rights Committee," *Netherlands Quarterly of Human Rights*, 41 no. 2 (2023), 97–114.

Barendt, Eric, *Academic Freedom and the Law: A Comparative Study*. Oxford: Hart, 2010.

Beaud, Olivier, "Reflections on the Concept of Academic Freedom," *European Review of History*, 27 no. 5 (2020), 611–627.

Belfast Guidelines on Amnesty and Accountability. Belfast: University of Ulster Transitional Justice Institute, 2013.

Bevir, Mark, *The Logic of the History of Ideas*. Cambridge: Cambridge University Press, 1999.

Bloxham, Donald, *History & Morality*. Oxford: Oxford University Press, 2020.

Bredin, Jean-Denis, "Le Droit, le juge et l'historien," *Le Débat*, no. 32 (November 1984), 93–111.

Brettschneider, Corey, *When the State Speaks, What Should It Say? How Democracies Can Protect Expression and Promote Equality*. Princeton, NJ: Princeton University Press, 2012.

Bublitz, Christoph, and Martin Dresler, "A Duty to Remember, a Right to Forget? Memory Manipulations and the Law," in *Handbook of Neuroethics*, eds. Jens Clausen and Neil Levy. Dordrecht: Springer, 2015, 1279–1307.

Burger, Peter, "The Berne Convention: Its History and Its Key Role in the Future," *Journal of Law and Technology*, 3 no. 1 (Winter 1988), 1–69.

Cassell, Douglas, "Steering Clear of the Twin Shoals of a Rights-Based Morality and a Duty-Based Legality," in *Between Rights and Responsibilities: A Fundamental Debate*, eds. Stephan Parmentier, Hans Werdmölder, and Michaël Merrigan. Cambridge: Intersentia, 2016, 51–65.

Centre for Law and Democracy, *Reconceptualising Copyright: Adapting the Rules to Respect Freedom of Expression in the Digital Age*. Halifax: CLD, 2013.

De Baets, Antoon, "Democracy and Historical Writing," *Historiografías/ Historiographies: The Journal of History and Theory*, no. 9 (June 2015), 31–43.

"A Historian's View on the Right to Be Forgotten," *International Review of Law, Computers and Technology*, 30 nos. 1–2 (March–July 2016), 57–66.

"Historians and Human Rights Advocacy," in *The Professional Historian in Public: Old and New Roles Revisited*, eds. Lutz Raphael and Berber Bevernage. Berlin: De Gruyter, 2023a, 299–325.

"Laws Governing the Historian's Free Expression," in *The Palgrave Handbook of State-Sponsored History after 1945*, eds. Berber Bevernage and Nico Wouters. London: Palgrave-Macmillan, 2018, 39–67.

"Memory and Tradition as Limits to the Freedom of Expression about the Past," *Storia della Storiografia/History of Historiography*, 79 no. 1 (September 2021), 19–42.

"The Posthumous Dignity of Dead Persons," in *Anthropology of Violent Death: Theoretical Foundations for Forensic Humanitarian Action*, eds. Roberto Parra and Douglas Ubelaker. Hoboken NJ: Wiley, 2023b, 15–37.

Responsible History. New York: Berghahn, 2009.

"The United Nations Human Rights Committee's View of the Past," in *Law and Memory: Towards Legal Governance of History*, eds. Uladzislau Belavusau and Aleksandra Gliszczyńska-Grabias. Cambridge: Cambridge University Press, 2017, 29–47.

"The View of the Past in International Humanitarian Law (1860–2020)," *International Review of the Red Cross*, 104 nos. 920–921 (November 2022), 1586–1620.

Dennett, Daniel, *Intuition Pumps and Other Tools for Thinking*. London: Penguin, 2014.

Dworkin, Ronald, *Justice for Hedgehogs*. Cambridge, MA: The Belknap Press of Harvard University Press, 2011.

Elias, T. O., "The Doctrine of Intertemporal Law," *American Journal of International Law*, 74 no. 2 (1980), 285–307.

Finlayson, James Gordon, *Habermas: A Very Short Introduction*. Oxford: Oxford University Press, 2005.

Foqué, René, "Human Rights and Human Responsibilities: Setting the Ethical and the Conceptual Scene," in *Between Rights and Responsibilities: A Fundamental Debate*, eds. Stephan Parmentier, Hans Werdmölder, and Michaël Merrigan. Cambridge: Intersentia, 2016, 13–34.

Frankfurt, Harry, *On Truth*. New York: Knopf, 2017.

Gibbons, Tony, "The Concept of Integrity," in *Integrity and Historical Research*, eds. Tony Gibbons and Emily Sutherland. London: Routledge, 2012, 1–12.

Gorman, Jonathan, "Ethics and the Writing of Historiography," in *A Companion to the Philosophy of History and Historiography*, ed. Aviezer Tucker. Chichester: Wiley-Blackwell, 2009, 253–261.

Gutman, Yifat, and Jenny Wüstenberg (eds.), *The Routledge Handbook of Memory Activism*. London: Routledge, 2023.

Halme-Tuomisaari, Miia, and Pamela Slotte, "Introduction," in *Revisiting the Origins of Human Rights*, eds. Pamela Slotte and Miia Halme-Tuomisaari. Cambridge: Cambridge University Press, 2015, 1–36.

Hammer, Leonard, *The International Human Right to Freedom of Conscience: An Approach to Its Application and Development*. London: SOAS, 1997.

Hazan, Pierre, *Amnesty: A Blessing in Disguise? Making Good Use of an Important Mechanism in Peace Processes*. Geneva: Centre for Humanitarian Dialogue, 2020.

Higgins, Rosalyn, "Time and the Law: International Perspectives on an Old Problem," *International and Comparative Law Quarterly*, 46 no. 3 (1997), 501–520.

Hoffmann, Stefan-Ludwig, "Human Rights and History," *Past and Present*, no. 232 (August 2016), 279–310.

International Committee of Historical Sciences, Constitution (1926, as amended in 1992 and 2005).

International Council on Archives, Universal Declaration on Archives (2010).

Jaspers, Karl, *The Question of German Guilt*, translation E. B. Ashton. New York: Fordham University Press, 2000 (originally German, 1947).

Jay, Martin, "Historical Truth and the Truthfulness of Historians," in *Integrity, Honesty, and Truth Seeking*, eds. Christian Miller and Ryan West. Oxford: Oxford University Press, 2020, 240–273.

Juzgado Federal de Resistencia, Expediente: FRE 9846/2019, "Masacre de Napalpí s/Juicio por la Verdad" (30 June 2022).

Kelsen, Hans, "The Rule against Ex Post Facto Laws and the Prosecution of the Axis War Criminals," *Judge Advocate Journal*, 2 no. 3 (1945), 8–12, 46.

"Will the Judgment in the Nuremberg Trial Constitute a Precedent in International Law?" *International Law Quarterly*, 1 no. 2 (1947), 153–171.

Kennedy, David, "The International Human Rights Movement: Part of the Problem?" *Harvard Human Rights Journal*, 15 (2002), 101–126.

"The International Human Rights Regime: Still Part of the Problem?" in *Examining Critical Perspectives on Human Rights*, eds. Rob Dickinson, Elena Katselli, Colin Murray, and Ole W. Pedersen. Cambridge: Cambridge University Press, 2012, 19–34.

Koskenniemi, Martti, "The Past According to International Law: A Practice of History and Histories of a Practice," in *History, Politics, Law: Thinking Internationally*, eds. Annabel Brett, Megan Donaldson, and Martti Koskenniemi. Cambridge: Cambridge University Press, 2021, 49–68.

Loth, Marc, "How Does Tort Law Deal with Historical Injustice? On Slavery Reparations, Post-Colonial Redress, and the Legitimations of Tort Law," *Journal of European Tort Law*, 11 no. 3 (2020), 181–207.

Maastricht Guidelines on Violations of Economic, Social and Cultural Rights (1997).

Mälksoo, Maria (ed.), *Handbook on the Politics of Memory*. Cheltenham: Elgar, 2023.

Meltzer, Bernard, "A Note on the Nuremberg Debate," *University of Chicago Law Review*, 14 no. 3 (April 1947), 455–469.

Mendel, Toby, "Emilio Palacio Urrutia and others versus Ecuador: Expert Statement by Toby Mendel." Halifax: Centre for Law and Democracy, 2021.

"Negotiating the Delicate Boundary between History and Hate Speech," *Storia della Storiografia/History of Historiography*, 79 no. 1 (2021), 43–63.

"Reflections on Media Self-Regulation: Lessons for Historians," *Storia della Storiografia/History of Historiography*, nos. 59–60 (September 2011), 50–65.

Mill, John Stuart, *On Liberty*. London: Longmans, Green & Co, 1865 (originally 1859).

Mokhtar, Aly, "Nullum Crimen, Nulla Poena sine Lege: Aspects and Prospects," *Statute Law Review*, 26 no. 1 (2005), 41–55.

Moynihan, Harriet, "Regulating the Past: The European Court of Human Rights' Approach to the Investigation of Historical Deaths under Article

2 ECHR," in *British Yearbook of International Law*. Oxford: Oxford University Press, 2016, 68–100.

Nowak, Manfred, *U.N. Covenant on Civil and Political Rights: CCPR Commentary*. Kehl: Engel, 2005 (second edition).

O'Flaherty, Michael, "Freedom of Expression: Article 19 of the International Covenant on Civil and Political Rights and the Human Rights Committee's General Comment No 34," *Human Rights Law Review*, 12 no. 4 (2012a), 627–654.

"Limitations on Freedom of Opinion and Expression: Growing Consensus or Hidden Faultlines?" *Proceedings of the Annual Meeting (American Society of International Law)*, 106 (2012b), 347–349.

Oreskes, Naomi, *Why Trust Science?* Princeton, NJ: Princeton University Press, 2019.

Parisi, Piergiuseppe, "The Obligation to Criminalise Historical Denialism in a Multilevel Human Rights System," in *Responsibility for Negation of International Crimes*, ed. Patrycja Grzebyk. Warsaw: Institute of Justice, 2020, 41–53.

Paul, Herman, *Historians' Virtues: From Antiquity to the Twenty-First Century*. Cambridge: Cambridge University Press, 2022.

Popper, Karl, *The Poverty of Historicism*. London: Harper and Row, 1957.

Post, Robert, *Constitutional Domains: Democracy, Community, Management*. Cambridge, MA: Harvard University Press, 1995.

Radbruch, Gustav, "Statutory Lawlessness and Supra-Statutory Law," *Oxford Journal of Legal Studies*, 26 no. 1 (2006), 1–11 (originally German, 1946).

Raphael, Lutz, and Benjamin Zachariah, "Intellectual Honesty and the Purposes of History," *Bloomsbury History: Theory and Method*. London: Bloomsbury Publishing, 2021.

Salojärvi, Juhana Mikael, "Human Rights in Time: Temporalization of Human Rights in Historical Representation," in *International Law and Time: Narratives and Techniques*, eds. Klara Polackova-Van der Ploeg, Luca Pasquet, and León Castellanos-Jankiewicz. Cham: Springer, 2022, 51–70.

Schabas, William, "Time, Justice, and Human Rights: Statutory Limitation on the Right to Truth?" in *Understanding the Age of Transitional Justice: Crimes, Courts, Commissions, and Chronicling*, ed. Nanci Adler. New Brunswick, NJ: Rutgers University Press, 2018, 37–55.

Sen, Amartya, "Democracy as a Universal Value," *Journal of Democracy*, 10 no. 3 (1999), 3–17.

Sunstein, Cass, "Analogical Reasoning and Precedent," *Philosophical Foundations of Precent*, eds. Timothy Endicott, Hafstein Dan Kristjánsson, and Sebastian Lewis. Oxford: Oxford University Press, 2023, 227–239.

Legal Reasoning and Political Conflict. Oxford: Oxford University Press, 2014.

Superior Court of the State of California, Mermelstein *versus* Institute for Historical Review (1991), www.concernedhistorians.org/le/579.pdf.

Tirosh, Noam, and Anna Reading (eds.), *The Right to Memory: History, Media, Law and Ethics*. New York: Berghahn, 2023.

Tshwane Principles: Global Principles on National Security and the Right to Information. New York: Open Society Foundations, 2013.

Tucker, Aviezer, "Historiographic Revision and Revisionism: The Evidential Difference," *Past in the Making: Historical Revisionism in Central Europe after 1989*, ed. Michal Kopeček. Budapest: Central European University Press, 2008, 1–15.

Weber, Max, *Wissenschaft als Beruf*. Munich: Duncker & Humboldt, 1919.

Wheatley, Steven, "Revisiting the Doctrine of Intertemporal Law," *Oxford Journal of Legal Studies*, 41 no. 2 (2021), 484–509.

Williams, Bernard, *Truth & Truthfulness: An Essay in Genealogy*. Princeton, NJ: Princeton University Press, 2002.

de Zayas, Alfred, and Áurea Roldán Martín, "Freedom of Opinion and Freedom of Expression: Some Reflections on General Comment No. 34 of the UN Human Rights Committee," *Netherlands International Law Review*, 59 no. 3 (September 2012), 425–454.

About the Author

Antoon De Baets is emeritus professor of History, Ethics, and Human Rights at the University of Groningen, the Netherlands. He is the author of publications on the censorship of history, the ethics of historians, and the history of human rights, among others. He is founder–coordinator of the Network of Concerned Historians, President of the International Commission for the History and Theory of Historiography, member of the Academia Europaea, and chair of the Scientific Advisory Committee of the project "The Netherlands and Afghanistan 2001–2021." A complete curriculum vitae is available at www .concernedhistorians.org/va/cv.pdf. His ORCID is 0000-0002-5734-8193.

Acknowledgments

This Element has long been in the making and I am grateful to many colleagues who provided critical comments on versions of sections of this text at conferences in Amsterdam, Bern, Bielefeld, Bologna, Brussels, Caen, Cergy, Cork, Firenze, Ghent, Groningen, The Hague, Hannover, Helsingør, Kristiansand, Lausanne, La Habana, Lisbon, Novara, Prague, Pune, Rome, Santiago de Compostela, Strasbourg, Utrecht, and Valletta. Toby Mendel, Dina Khapaeva, and two anonymous reviewers deserve special thanks. I am much indebted to Daniel Woolf for his encouragement.

Cambridge Elements ≡

Historical Theory and Practice

Daniel Woolf

Queen's University, Ontario

Daniel Woolf is Professor of History at Queen's University, where he served for ten years as Principal and Vice-Chancellor, and has held academic appointments at a number of Canadian universities. He is the author or editor of several books and articles on the history of historical thought and writing, and on early modern British intellectual history, including most recently *A Concise History of History* (CUP 2019). He is a Fellow of the Royal Historical Society, the Royal Society of Canada, and the Society of Antiquaries of London. He is married with 3 adult children.

About the Series

Cambridge Elements in Historical Theory and Practice is a series intended for a wide range of students, scholars, and others whose interests involve engagement with the past. Topics include the theoretical, ethical, and philosophical issues involved in doing history, the interconnections between history and other disciplines and questions of method, and the application of historical knowledge to contemporary global and social issues such as climate change, reconciliation and justice, heritage, and identity politics.

Cambridge Elements ☰

Historical Theory and Practice

Elements in the Series

A full series listing is available at: www.cambridge.org/EHTP

Printed in the United States
by Baker & Taylor Publisher Services